The collector's all-colour guide to

TOY
Soldiers

A record of the world's miniature armies: from 1850 to the present day

The collector's all-colour guide to
TOY Soldiers

A record of the world's miniature armies: from 1850 to the present day

Andrew Rose

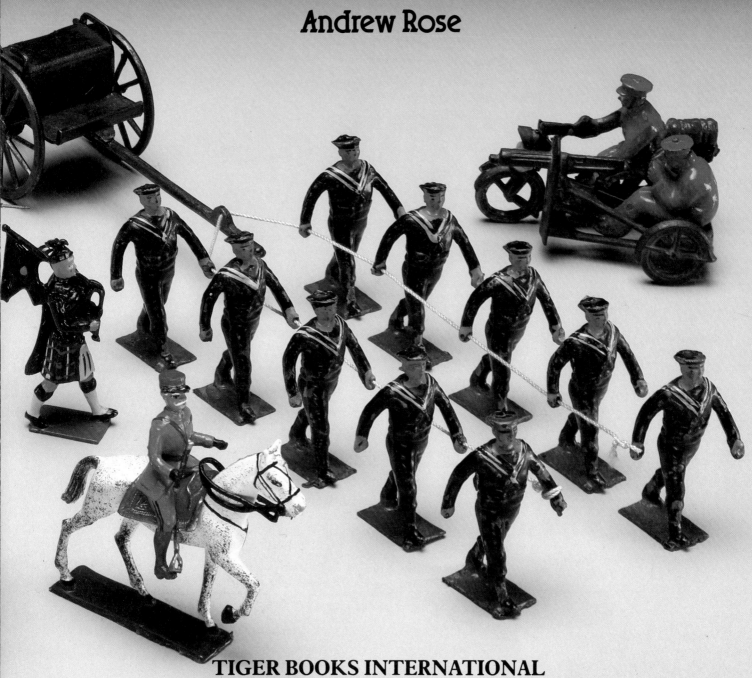

TIGER BOOKS INTERNATIONAL
LONDON

A Salamander Book

Acknowledgements

This edition published in 1989 by
Tiger Books International PLC, London.

© Salamander Books Ltd 1985

ISBN 1 85501 023 2

Editor:
John Woodward

Designer:
Barry Savage

Photography:
Terry Dilliway
© Salamander Books Ltd.

Filmset:
Instep Print & Design Ltd.

Colour reproduction:
Melbourne Graphics

Printed in Belgium.

Special thanks, both for the generous loan of many items for photography, and for
much invaluable advice, are due to:

Major E. Roche-Kelly

Special thanks for the loan of toy soldiers, information on aluminium figures, and
facilities for photography are due to:

Giles Brown and **Paula Caira**
Dorset Soldiers, 42 Nettlecombe, Shaftesbury, Dorset

For the loan of toy soldiers for photography, thanks to:

R. V. Archard

G. Baker

Jeanne Burley
340 Upper Montagu Street, London W1

Pierce Carlson
Grays Mews, Davies Street, London W1

Jock Coutts
"Under Two Flags", 4 St Christopher's Place, London W1

R. J. Dew and **R. P. Dew**

J. G. Garratt

Peter Flataus
Stall 30, 290 Westbourne Grove, London W11

H. Taylor

Len Taylor
Trophy Miniatures, Unit 11, Barry Workshops, Sully Moors Road, Sully,
Penarth, South Wales

Coralie Wearing

And for information and advice, thanks to:

James Opie

Contents

Introduction

Miniature figures of fighting men have been produced for over 4,000 years. They were not always intended as playthings: the figures placed in the tombs of Ancient Egyptian Pharaohs represented the troops and servants who would accompany the departed in the after-life — the first Emperor of China had full-size terracotta figures to fulfil this purpose. From the medieval period onwards young princes were given armies of miniature soldiers which were often made in precious metals; although primarily intended to be educational, for the study of drill and tactics, they were quite probably also put to less serious purposes.

The earliest lead toy soldiers to be found date from Roman times, but the toy soldier as we know it today, by definition an item intended primarily as a children's plaything and "mass produced" to some degree, originated in the *Zinnfiguren* or flat tin figures produced in Germany from the 1730s onwards by the tinsmiths of Nuremberg, at first as a sideline to pewter ware or jewellery making. Pastoral

scenes of farming and hunting, festivities and religious ceremonies were portrayed as well as soldiers. These finely engraved figures, only 1mm (0.04in) or less thick, were cast from slate moulds in a variety of sizes — although many makers later standardized on the 30mm (1.18in) Nuremberg scale introduced by Heinrichsen (see *pages 20-21*).

The semi-flat figure, which also originated in Germany, was bulkier than the flat and had a higher lead content. The engraving was less fine, and although excellent and charming semi-flat figures have been produced, some of the poorest of all toy soldiers, with little to recommend them, were made in this style. (See *pages 22-23*).

Fully-round solid lead figures appeared towards the end of the 18th century in Paris, the first identifiable maker being Lucotte, whose moulds still survive in the hands of C.B.G. Mignot (see *pages 24-29*). In Germany the most prolific manufacturer of solid lead figures was Georg Heyde, who began production in about 1870. Unable to break that country's allegiance to the flat figure, he neverthe-

less had considerable success with exports, especially to Great Britain and the USA (see *pages 30-33*).

Until the 1890s toy soldier production in Great Britain was negligible. The UK market relied on imports, principally from Heyde and other German manufacturers, and to a lesser extent from Lucotte and Mignot of France. This situation was to change dramatically when the established toy-making firm of William Britain started to produce lead toy soldiers using the hollow-casting technique in 1893. Lighter and cheaper to transport, as well as somehow more aesthetically pleasing, these new soldiers soon caught on — at first ousting many of the foreign imports and then being widely exported themselves. Hollow-cast soldiers — predominantly by Britains, but also by many other smaller firms — became the principal type in the English-speaking world and are now the most widely collected.

In Germany and some other European countries "composition" soldiers, made from a mixture of sawdust, plaster and glue, achieved some

Above: *An early Britains RHA gun team, and a Mignot 1914 line infantry band.*

Above: *The majority of the toy soldiers illustrated in this book are to 1:32 scale or "standard" size, infantry figures being approximately 54mm (2.12in) high from the base to the top of the head (without headgear). Where figures of a smaller or larger size are shown this "standard" size Britains Royal Welsh Fusilier from set 2124 is used to indicate the scale.*

popularity. The composition figures made by the firms Hausser-Elastolin and Lineol were particularly well-modelled (see *pages 120-121*).

In the inter-war period the production of aluminium toy soldiers was developed in France, with some pleasing results. After World War II the firm of Wend-Al made aluminium soldiers in Great Britain for a while, until competition from plastic became too strong (see *pages 122-123*).

In the post-war period the demise of the hollow-cast lead toy soldier became inevitable following the great increase in the cost of metal, the advent of toy safety regulations and the development of "unbreakable" plastic figures. The first attempt at marketing plastic injection-moulded toy soldiers in Great Britain was made in 1947 by Malleable Mouldings of Deal, Kent, but this soon failed. The most innovative and successful manufacturer of plastic figures was the partnership of M. Zang and R. Selwyn-Smith which started production in 1951, adopting the name "Herald" in 1953. Associated with Britains from 1955 they became fully

incorporated in 1958. In the 1950s Herald led the expanding field of plastic toy soldier production, now 30 years on greatly reduced by the loss of such famous names as Johillco, Crescent and Timpo.

Early plastic figures in particular were often finely detailed and imaginative in design. Unfortunately parents and children took the "unbreakable" nature of plastics rather literally, and these soldiers were often not as well looked-after as their lead counterparts. Furthermore the technology to produce paint that would adhere well to flexible plastics had not been perfected, resulting in problems with paint flaking off. As a result many early plastic figures are much harder to find in mint condition than older lead soldiers (see *pages 124-125*).

BRITAINS FIGURES

It will be noted that the products of one particular manufacturer, Britains Ltd, dominate the pages of this book. This company was the first to apply the hollow-cast process to toy soldier production, and made a vast range of high-quality figures and associated equipment over a period of more than 70 years. These are now the most widely collected of all lead toy soldiers, internationally.

William Britain Snr had been producing mechanical tin toys in North London since the 1840s, but these were quite expensive items with limited sales. In 1893, aiming to break into the German-dominated toy soldier trade, the founder's son William Britain Jnr adopted the hollow casting technique — which had already been used in Germany for making other toys — for the production of toy soldiers. In this process an alloy of lead and antimony was poured into a brass mould and swiftly out again, leaving a thin cooling skin of metal over the surface of the mould and thus producing a hollow figure. The temperature, both of the molten metal and the mould, were critical. The great advantages of the technique were the saving in the quantity — and cost — of metal used, and the cheaper transport costs associated with the lighter hollow-cast figures.

Most Britains figures were to a scale of 1:32, an infantryman being 54mm (2.12in) high from his base to the top of his head (without head-dress). Known as "standard size", such figures were to the same scale as the Gauge 1 toy railways of the period. There were some anomalies in the early days, with oversized fusiliers and Scots Greys, and undersized lancers and infantrymen of the Royal Sussex Regiment. Some of the earliest figures are also regarded as being "Germanic" in appearance — perhaps because Britains were more concerned with perfecting the hollow-cast technique than with creating original designs when they first started.

Britains 54mm (2.12in) soldiers were usually sold in boxes of five cavalry or eight infantry, but until 1940 boxes of fixed-arm infantry, such as standing firing soldiers, contained ten figures. From 1960 most cavalry sets were reduced to four pieces, and infantry sets to seven. There were also Display Sets containing combinations of other sets, but sometimes including figures not otherwise obtainable.

At first the figures had fixed arms, with tin-strip swords for the cavalry, but these soon gave way to movable arms, each held in place with a rivet at the shoulder. Often these had little "play value", but they overcame the problem of a deep "undercut" in the casting, and also provided opportunities for varying the nature of the figures by using different movable arms on identical body castings.

Up to the turn of the century, bases were generally oval and unmarked. In

Above: *Printed paper sheets to be cut out and mounted on card were first produced in the mid 18th century. The items above, clockwise from left, are: French infantry of the line, 1880s uniform, by Pellerin of Épinal; Montenegrin infantry of 1914, by Pellerin; Italian Alpini of World War I by Pellerin — note these are double-sided figures; a Pellerin reprint of a pre-Revolutionary sheet of French Grenadiers of the Royal Guard; a World War I American Army first aid post by Pellerin; a selection of late Victorian British "scraps" including the Black Watch and some fanciful potrayals of women in uniform; a sheet of double-sided Chasseurs Alpins in horizon blue by an unknown* French maker; and riflemen produced by the British firm of Chad Valley in the 1950s, mounted on plywood with wooden bases and descriptions printed on the back.

Top right: *Figures by Lucotte and Mignot, those by Lucotte being on the left of each pair. Of the two British Waterloo-period infantrymen note the better modelling of the Lucotte figure. The arms are cast separately and located on lugs before soldering, while the Mignot arms are bent into position and the weapon soldered on. The Lucotte French 5th Hussar has movable reins and a detachable saddle with stirrups, while that of the Mignot Austrian Hussar is soldered on.*

1900 the new City Imperial Volunteers figure was the first to have a paper label on the base bearing the date and the words "copyright William Britains Jnr". Such paper labels were used for a few years, then dropped in favour of lettering engraved into the mould. One of the reasons for this step was the rise of a number of rivals to Britains in the 1900s, some of whom were not above "pirating" their designs and producing near-identical copies. Britains were to take a number of firms to court over this activity, publishing the results of these actions in their catalogues. In 1911 the Sculpture Copyright Act was changed, making dating of the designs unnecessary, and Britains ceased dating their figures in the following

year — although the dates were not immediately removed from existing Britains moulds.

From 1907 square or rectangular bases replaced the oval ones, although a few figures such as the medical officers and the charging Japanese infantry remained round-based throughout production.

The makers of solid figures, such as Mignot and Heyde, produced a large variety of different soldiers using a standard body by means of different "plug-in" heads. Britains achieved the same effect by having interchangeable head moulds that bolted on to the body mould; in this way the same body could represent, for example, an infantryman, a guardsman or a

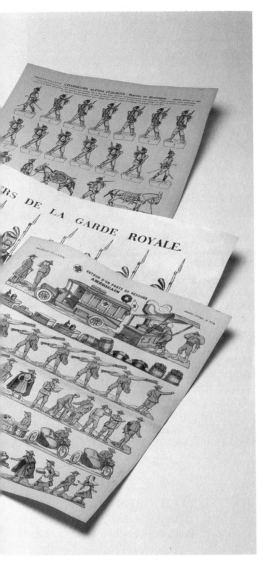

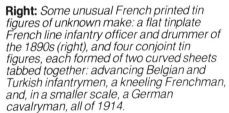

Right: *Some unusual French printed tin figures of unknown make: a flat tinplate French line infantry officer and drummer of the 1890s (right), and four conjoint tin figures, each formed of two curved sheets tabbed together: advancing Belgian and Turkish infantrymen, a kneeling Frenchman, and, in a smaller scale, a German cavalryman, all of 1914.*

Below right: *Britains bases, showing the early paper copyright labels of a Seaforth Highlander, set 112 (left), and a Russian infantryman, set 133 (centre). The base on the right is from a Royal Marine running at the trail, set 1284, of the 1950s.*

marine. The same casting could also be used to represent a completely different unit by a different paint finish.

Although better known and justly famous for their "standard" 54mm (2.12in) size figures, from 1896 until 1940 Britains produced a range of small-size figures, the infantry being about 44mm (1.73in) high and the cavalry 55mm (2.16in). They were originally included in the main catalogue listing, and only the fact that they were in boxes of four cavalry or seven infantry, and about half the price of the "standard" sets, revealed that they were small-size figures. There were also Display Sets. These undersized soldiers must have disappointed many children who had

ordered from the catalogue believing that they were "standard" figures!

The 44mm (1.73in) figures were soon listed separately, and known as the "B" series. The infantry were at first oval-based fixed-arm figures, but well modelled with deep undercuts and weapons held well away from the body. Most of the cavalry had movable arms, and both they and the infantry were painted to a good standard.

In the 1920s the "B" series changed to the "W" series, the cavalry being fixed-arm, and the infantry square-based, slimmer and fractionally taller with rifles at the slope moulded more closely to the body to make for ease of casting. The painting was second-grade. The change to the simplified castings occurred while the "B" series were still being produced, the more basic painting indicating a "W" series figure. The "W" range was at first very limited; infantry were available in boxes of six or 12, but there were also display boxes. (See *pages 92-93*).

In 1905 six sets of 54mm (2.12in) French troops were introduced, and the Paris Office was set up to help with the sale of these and all Britains figures. There was sufficient interest to open a Paris factory in 1912, which as well as the usual lines produced soldiers which were never available in England and are now highly collectable. The French operation lasted only until the early 1920s. Paris Office figures are marked "Deposé" on the base, but this mark can also be found on figures made from the Paris moulds after they were returned to London.

During World War I most of Britains' resources were devoted to making munitions, although soldier production did not cease entirely. After "the war to end wars" relatively few new figures based on that conflict were produced, with more emphasis on the delightful "Home Farm" series.

In the early 1930s the range was increased, mainly for export, and with re-armament a series of "modern army" troops was introduced, with motorized vehicles and anti-aircraft equipment. World War II put a stop to production for the duration, and many of the former glories of the catalogue were never to reappear.

In the immediate post-war period materials were in short supply and the UK needed dollars, so Britains concentrated on export only, mainly to the USA. The range began to expand again, the coronation of Queen Elizabeth II in 1953 resulting in a number of attractive sets. The short-lived half-size sets of four rather than eight figures, produced to a better standard, and the individual figures in the "Picture Pack" series were an attempt to attract serious collectors. The dwindling range was completely re-numbered in the "9000" series in 1962 and became almost exclusively export only. Hollow-cast toy soldier production finally came to an end in 1966.

JOHILLCO FIGURES

After Britains, the best-known maker of lead hollow-cast figures was John Hill & Co. of Islington, London, usually known as Johillco. The firm was founded *c*1900 by the Wood brothers, at least one of whom was a former employee of Britains.

Although considered by Britains as their greatest rival, figures made by Johillco up to the 1930s are quite hard to find; scarcer, for example, than figures by Reka. This was because they were producing toy and novelty items for other firms rather than concentrating solely on toy soldiers.

Johillco's range of soldiers was large but variable in quality, their best work being more individualistic and less "stiff" than some figures by Britains. Boxed sets by Johillco are quite scarce, as they placed more emphasis on selling figures singly. The castings were often available in several grades of paint finish; their best painting was comparable with that of Britains, but most of their soldiers are found in second-grade finish. They used the system of common body castings with different heads much less than Britains. (See *pages 108-111*).

After World War II Johillco re-emerged in Burnley, Lancashire, under new ownership, their London factory having been destroyed in the Blitz. They survived until the late 1950s, briefly producing plastic figures, now quite hard to find, marked "Hilco".

Top left: *Medical and nursing figures make an attractive theme for a small collection. In the foreground are wounded figures on stretchers by Britains. The unusual nurses in khaki and the wounded soldier walking with crutches are by Cherilea. The two standing nurses, left centre, are of unknown make; that on the right may be French. The small figure in dark grey is by Renvoize, with a nurse by Fry behind her on the right. The undersized standing nurse is by Crescent. The kneeling nurses are, left to right, by Johillco, Crescent and Johillco (a rarer version), while on the right are a group of five Britains nurses of various periods.*

Top right: *Toy soldier makers were quick to produce figures based on contemporary events. Like Britains, Johillco issued a number of interesting figures at the time of the Italian invasion of Abyssinia in 1935. In*

the foreground is the scarce Abyssinian mountain battery utilizing a mule and a small gun which was already available. Behind the battery an Abyssinian stretcher party is escorted by a squad of barefoot infantry. At the rear are tribesmen in assorted coloured robes, and rather undersized Italian infantry in tropical helmets.

Above: *Although the vast majority of British hollow-cast soldiers were made in 54mm (2.12in) size most makers produced a few large figures. From the left: an early Crescent C287 "Khaki Captain"; a marching movable-arm British infantryman by Hanks, dated 1912; a Johillco 575A marching khaki officer; a Johillco 577A Crusader with a 54mm Knight of St John, of exactly the same design; and three Crescent figures: C284 Life Guard, C277 Highlander and C282 Hindoo.*

OTHER COMPETITORS OF BRITAINS, 1890 TO 1930

This account of the early competitors of Britains has been compiled by Peter Cowan, a toy soldier maker and collector, and an acknowledged expert on the largely unmarked products of these little-known manufacturers.

Following Britains' adaptation of the German hollow-casting process to toy soldier production in the 1890s, and their swift rise to the premier position in the toy figure business, many other British toymakers sought to emulate them. Some, such as Charles W. Baker of Reka Ltd, and James S. Renvoize and Sons, were already established toy makers and wholesalers whose business had been adversely affected by Britains' inroads into the previously dominant German toy soldier sales. Others, such as the Woods brothers of Johillco and the Hanks brothers and their associate W.S. Sutton, were disaffected ex-employees of Britains who were determined to enter into business for themselves. Enterprising skilled craftsmen such as Arthur Fry of the Erecto Toy Co. and William Pickford of the Britannia Model Co. (later Soldarma) were also among those drawn to the market which Britains had developed.

Johillco were to last longer than any of Britains' other rivals, although until the 1930s the company's production was diversified away from exclusive

toy soldier manufacture and into castings, pressings and stampings for other toy and novelty makers. This diversification probably enabled the firm to survive the economic depression of the 1930s, during which most of their smaller, more specialized competitors went into liquidation. Relatively well-documented, and, in the case of the later figures, easy to find, Johillco soldiers have attracted more interest from collectors than items produced by the other rivals to Britains. Nevertheless, many of the toy soldiers produced by these lesser companies can still be found, and in some cases indentifiable figures have survived in sufficient numbers to form a very interesting collection.

Many small British companies, most located in north-east London, started toy figure production in the 1890s. Their earliest figures were frequently poorly executed and, bearing no identifying marks, surviving examples have proved impossible to attribute with certainty. Unlike Britains, who were renowned for their well-designed and illustrated catalogues, few other makers had extensive brochures and these few often restricted circulation to the retail trade shops; the brochures were not available to the public, usually being destroyed on the issue of a new list, or on the demise of the unfortunate company.

To some extent this handicap to identification is offset by the practice, increasingly common after 1900, of incorporating the trade-mark and country of origin on the base, or on an inconspicuous part of the figure itself.

This was partly an attempt to prevent other manufacturers "pirating" successful designs, and producing cheaper and usually inferior copies. Unfortunately the marking of figures in this way was by no means universal, and more laborious means of identifying figures must often be resorted to. Only research into patents, companies and local records, coupled with close examination of a large number of non-Britains figures in order to group similar designs and styles, has enabled the following early toy soldier makers to be identified.

C.D. Abel and Co., of Islington, London were active from 1898 to 1914. One of the smallest of Britains' competitors, Abel produced a consistently good figure comparable with Britains figures of the same period. Although

Above left: *Imperial Yeomanry by Renvoize and Britains, c1900. The left-hand figures are by Renvoize.*

Above: *From the Unity Toy series by O.H. & Co., c1920, a powerful gun responsible for many broken ranks, and a cheap range of target figures made for them by WTC.*

Above right: *Reka Royal Army Medical Corps figures with a casualty clearing station tent, c1920.*

Right: *Early Scots, c1900. The right-hand figure in each pair is a Hanks copy of the Britains original on its left.*

Left: *Indian cavalry by Britains (left) and a "pirate" by Hanks, c1900.*

Far left: *Madras Infantry by Renvoize (left) and Britains, c1899. Ironically the Martini-Henry rifle of the Renvoize figure is more accurate than that of the Britains figure.*

their oval or square bases are unmarked, many of the models have a distinctive inset brass socket for a parade-drill game patented by Abel in 1902. It is possible that some of Abel's designers worked for Reka after 1910. (See *pages 98-99*).

James S. Renvoize and Sons, of Stoke Newington, London were wholesalers and toy importers from the 1890s to 1914. Renvoize countered Britains' decimation of the German (solid-cast) toy soldier market by simply arranging for the production of similar hollow-casts by his existing suppliers. Whether intentionally or not, this resulted in the sale of well-made, well-finished sets which were little altered from the Britains originals — but at a lower price. This "piracy" became an increasing problem

to Britains until, in 1900, the company achieved the successful prosecution of several manufacturers, including Renvoize, by the use of a date-stamped copyright mark incorporated on the design — in this case an Imperial Yeoman. Following the outbreak of World War I Renvoize, like most patriotic British firms, ceased importing German toys, and even though they were by then producing some sets in the United Kingdom, they did not resume the sale of lead toys after the war. (See *pages 100-101*).

Hanks Brothers of Hackney, London, traded from 1897 to 1917. Previously employees of Britains, the Hanks brothers and their colleague Walter Sutton were the "Pirate Kings" of the toy soldier world, until their activities were curtailed by the

restrictions imposed on metal toys during World War I. Concentrating on the pre-copyrighted designs of Britains, along with some less inspired designs of their own, Hanks were a constant thorn in the flesh of Britains. Many apparently early but uncatalogued sets of cavalry by Britains have been found to be by Hanks. After the war a new company formed with Sutton struggled along until its final demise in the depression of 1920s. (See *pages 100-101*).

Reka Ltd, of Islington, London, produced toy soldiers from 1908 to 1930. The company was formed by another toy wholesaler, C.W. Baker, who had been offering a range of toy soldiers "made in Great Britain exclusively for us" since the early 1900s. These may have been made by Johillco, as G.

Wood of that company was responsible for some of Reka's designs after 1910, by which time they were manufacturing for themselves from their factory near Essex Road in North London. By the 1920s Reka's range had expanded considerably, and in volume of production they were probably second only to Britains and ahead of Johillco (see *pages 102-105*). In 1922, however, at the time of Reka's largest capital investment in new moulds, a trade magazine reported that "toy soldiers were a drug on the Christmas market" — the urgent clamouring for war toys in the opening years of World War I had been replaced by a public revulsion towards these small reminders of the useless carnage. Accordingly Baker gradually redirected his efforts towards other areas of his business, and in 1930 he sold most of his remaining working moulds to Crescent Ltd, of Tottenham in north London.

This small firm, which had been operating on the fringes of the toy and novelty market since 1925, was thereby given a cheap inroad to wider sales, and survived beyond Reka's eventual closure in 1940. Crescent seem to have bought in most of their moulds from other firms, as their range tends to lack consistency of style. After World War II the company successfully made the transition to plastic figure manufacture, and they also produced a rather limited but excellent range of diecast metal artillery pieces. (See *pages 112-113*).

The Erecto Toy Co. (Fry's Fighting Soldiers) was formed by the two Fry brothers and R. Hollyer in May 1915, in response to the huge wartime demand for model soldiers. By concentrating on the Allied forces, and making lively figures which owed nothing to any other manufacturer's designs, they captured a large part of the available market. Sadly, as with many other companies, by 1922 the reversed fortunes of the toy soldier market had caused them to go into liquidation. (see *pages 98-99*.)

Above: *A Taylor & Barrett infantryman presents arms to a group of women in uniform. From the left they are: a Britains nurse in khaki — although listed as such she is more often found as a WAAF; an ATS girl by Crescent, apparently designed to carry something in her right hand, and the only female steel-helmeted lead figure known; a rare ATS figure by Taylor & Barrett — a similar bugle-playing figure at attention has also been found; and a Cherilea ATS girl at "eyes left".*

Top right: *Two examples of boxed sets by Crescent, from the 1950s. That in the foreground contains small Scots Greys figures as shown. The large open box of "Medieval Knights" contains an assortment of figures covering a large historical period. Note the modern Household Cavalry state trumpeter masquerading as a herald!*

Right: *The short-lived Fylde Manufacturing Co., which commenced production c1946 and was absorbed by Cherilea in 1950, produced rather indifferent derivative figures in the main. This interesting boxed set of Waterloo period Black Watch Highlanders is a remarkable exception.*

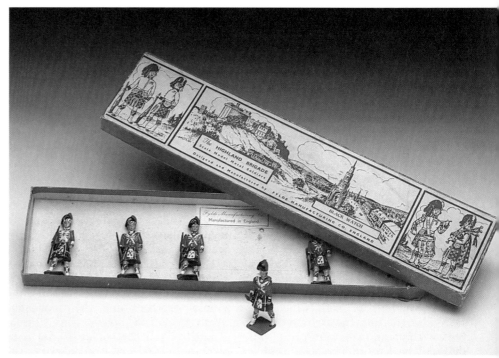

Another of Britains' competitors, Soldarma, originated in 1919 when, following the raising of the restriction on lead toy production, W.S. Pickford started production of an excellent range of large-scale model figures trading as The Britannia Model Co. of Hoxton, London. Johillco, who had already registered the trade-mark "Britannia Brand" from their address in Britannia Row, Islington, objected strongly to this, and by May 1920 Pickford was using the name Sold-arma and selling the compromise "BMC Series" (see *pages 106-107*.) By concentrating on high-quality, well-made and well-presented boxes of figures, and by diversifying into the cowboys and Indians depicted in the then-popular cinema films, they were able to weather the rough period of the 1920s — but the company eventually foundered during the greater depression of the 1930s.

LATER COMPETITORS OF BRITAINS

Although the majority of Britains' competitors went into decline in the 1920s and 1930s, a few more did spring up to take their place. Figures by all these makers are illustrated on *pages 112-113*.

The London firm of Charbens was founded by a former employee of Britains during the 1920s, and produced hollow-cast, rather second-quality figures and some interesting civilian vehicles. Their later figures, which included GIs and medieval knights, were rather reminiscent of Timpo. Charbens survived until 1968, latterly producing plastic figures which were largely derived from their earlier hollow-cast range with the old moulds suitably adapted for the new injection moulding process.

Taylor & Barrett, also of London, produced some slightly under 54mm (2.12in) size hollow-cast soldiers and sailors, as well as a range of civilian items and vehicles, from the late 1920s. The figures were marked "T & B". When the partnership split up one half became F.G. Taylor & Sons, and later issued a range of plastic farm items, while the other became Barrett & Sons, continuing to make a variety of soldiers which were marked on the base with a capital "B".

Cherilea Products were founded in Blackpool, Lancashire in 1948, and produced rather simple hollow-cast figures, some of which were very similar to Johillco products. In 1950 they took over the Fylde Manufacturing Co., also of Blackpool. Cherilea later brought out a wide range of plastic soldiers, usually rather over 54mm (2.12in) "standard" size. These were noted more for their vigorous and often dramatic poses than for the accuracy of their uniform detail.

WHAT TO COLLECT

When forming a collection it is probably best to stick to a theme, or themes. This may be the work of a particular maker — although in the case of Britains that would be a daunting task — or soldiers in a particular material, or from a specific period or country. There is a special appeal about a set of toy soldiers in their original box; perhaps it is something to do with reliving a child's pleasure and delight on discovering the shiny row of soldiers within. Whatever the reason, some collectors are only interested in figures in their original boxes, and the presence of the original packaging can increase the value of a set of soldiers by 50 per cent or more over their unboxed state. Others like to collect as many single figure variations and versions as possible, or even hundreds of the same figure to form a complete regiment on parade.

The hollow-cast production of a firm such as Britains, although enormous, is fairly well documented, so one is on fairly safe ground dealing with set numbers and versions. In the case of lesser known makers there is still plenty of scope for original research, along the lines carried out by Peter Cowan in his contribution to this book. There is still much research to be done, perhaps by a French collector, into the range of figures produced by Britains' Paris Office, and into the many French hollow-cast figures that the Paris operation may have inspired.

IDENTIFICATION OF FIGURES

Where the soldier is marked with the maker's name there is little problem. All Britains figures from the 1900s onwards are marked, as are most, but not all, Johillco figures.

Above: *Spanish soldiers from the 1940s. On the left is the packaging for a series called "The Military History of Spain" issued by Multicolor of Madrid. Each little "book" contained one cavalryman or two infantrymen — the figures shown are a pair of stretcher bearers. On the right are 30mm (1.18in) war game figures with movable arms, and a tank and anti-tank gun, all produced by Sanquez in co-operation with the Spanish Army Ministry.*

Right: *Makers' catalogues are a useful source for identifying and dating figures. Shown here, clockwise from top left, are: the Britains "New Lines" supplement for 1957, illustrating the short-lived "half sets" containing three or four figures; a Britains 1960 catalogue which still had a good range of lead figures as well as plastics; a Britains authorized reprint of a large catalogue of c1915; a "pocket edition" of the 1958 Britains catalogue, which illustrates the Picture Pack series and is available in a larger format as a reprint; a reprinted Johillco catalogue from c1934; the very last edition Britains lead soldier catalogue from 1966; a compilation of reprints from several Crescent catalogues; the Britains catalogue for 1939, also available as a reprint; and one of two Cherilea catalogues of the mid-1950s obtainable as a reprint.*

Early Britains are very well painted, with details such as eyebrows and moustaches, and a quite dark skin colour. Horses have pink noses. Moustaches were discontinued from about 1940, mouths being indicated by a small splash of red. Post-war painting tends to be simpler, and the skin colour is a creamier shade.

Identification of an unmarked piece can often be made by comparing the style with that of a soldier of known make. Even the style in which, for example, "Made in England" is written on the base of a figure can be a valuable clue. To familiarize oneself with different makes there is no real substitute for seeing and, where possible, handling as many figures as

one can, whether in private collections, museums or by viewing at auctions.

Another useful aid to identification is by reference to makers' catalogues. Originals are now very hard to find, but a number of reprints of Britains catalogues are available from specialist dealers, as well as examples of brochures issued by Johillco, Crescent, Timpo, Charbens and Cherilea.

Obviously whenever possible the collector will want to acquire figures in near—perfect condition, but in the case of rare figures and/or limited financial resources, this may not always be possible. The price for a figure in scratched or damaged condition should be considerably less than that for a pristine example — something of

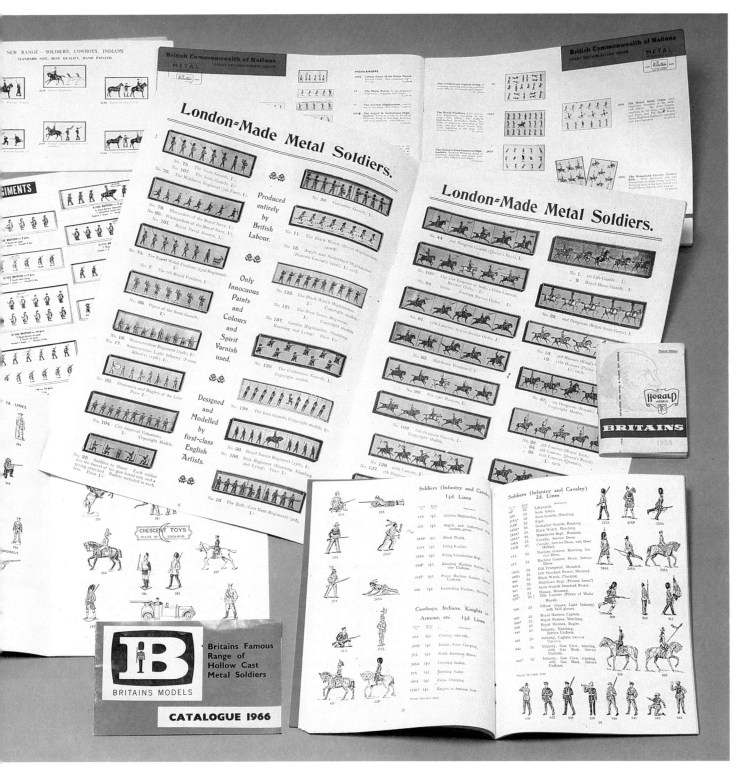

which not all non-specialist dealers seem to be aware! In the case of the rarest figures it is probably best to leave them in exactly the condition as found. With less rare figures in poor condition the collector may feel it is worthwhile carrying out a little restoration work.

RESTORATION AND STORAGE

It is now possible to buy recast replacement parts such as arms, heads and horses' legs for many figures by Britains and some other makers. With these, and some care in repainting — preferably with a good condition original figure as a reference — a satisfactory result can be obtained. But some words of caution: if the figures are repainted it should be done for one's own satisfaction and to fill a gap in a collection; if the items are later sold it is only fair to indicate to the potential purchaser the amount of restoration work carried out. Conversely, when buying toy soldiers the possibility of repainting having taken place should be looked into and the price adjusted accordingly — one collector's beautifully repainted figures may be only worth the value of the castings to another.

The main problem with the preservation of lead toy toy figures is the formation of lead sulphide, commonly known as "lead disease" or "lead rot", caused by the reaction of the lead with sulphur in the atmosphere and greatly accelerated by the presence of moisture. In its early stages this shows as a grey powdery surface to exposed metal parts such as bases and bayonets. In more advanced cases the figure will have a rough and brittle feel and will ultimately disintegrate. The best cure for lead disease is to avoid damp storage conditions. Do not use totally sealed cabinets for displaying figures, and use absorbent materials such as tissue paper and cardboard when packing figures away — not plastics. When buying, avoid seriously "diseased" items, but figures with slight discoloration are acceptable, should be cheaper, and will not deteriorate further if properly looked after and kept away from damp.

Top: *A typical bronze mould for producing hollow-cast figures. This particular tool is a Taylor & Barrett mould of the 1930s which produces a Guardsman at attention. From left to right: The two halves of the mould are hinged together by the handles. When it is open the small vent at the head end of the cavity can be seen; this allows for the displacement of air when the molten metal is tipped in and the surplus poured out. As the mould is closed a pouring funnel is swung into position ready for casting. The lead alloy is poured in, the surplus expelled by a flick of the wrist, and the pouring funnel slid off; it scrapes the base of the figure clean and flat as it moves across. Opening the mould reveals the new casting, ready to be cleaned up and painted. A skilled worker can make 150 figures per hour in this way.*

Below: *The Taylor & Barrett mould shown above was used to produce figures for set 2015: The Changing of the Guard — here shown with a newly-cast Guardsman.*

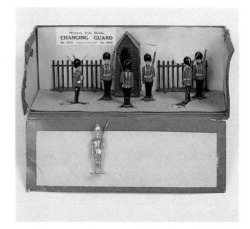

A problem that can affect most types of toy soldier is that of paint fading. To combat this, figures on display should be protected from direct sunlight.

DEGREES OF RARITY

Rarity in collecting is a combination of the scarcity of an item and its desirability. A toy soldier can only be desired and sought after if its existence is documented. As the production history of Britains Ltd. is now fairly well recorded and their products are widely collected one is on fairly sure ground with the relative availability and demand for different sets.

All pre-World War I Britains figures in good condition can be regarded as fairly scarce simply because of their age. Nevertheless, soldiers produced much more recently, but for a shorter time and in smaller quantities, can be equally hard to obtain. A set that was probably not very popular at the time and not a good seller — such as the Montenegrin Infantry — now commands a high price. On the other hand, the wide interest in the colour and spectacle of military bands means that all Britains bands, however common in terms of numbers produced, fetch a comparatively good price.

In this book no attempt has been made to give a relative rarity value to every single figure; the rarest and some of the commonest have been noted, the rest falling into a middle grouping of average availability, which can vary with where the collector happens to live. Early Britains figures are probably more readily available in their country of origin than in the USA, but the soldiers produced almost exclusively for export in the post-World War II period may be more common in the USA.

In the case of the smaller and less well-documented makers the situation is rather different — their products are much scarcer but far fewer people collect or can identify them. In the course of producing this book the author has acquired several previously unknown and unidentified figures, which arguably are very rare, but they only cost pennies because they have no established rarity value.

Try to avoid regarding toy soldiers as an investment, for such an attitude can only force prices up. Toy collecting should be fun, and the more collectors who can afford to enjoy it, the better.

Left: *Since 1945 most solid lead figures have been produced using centrifugal moulds. The master figures are sandwiched radially between black rubber discs and subjected to heat and pressure in a press, so that their impressions are vulcanized into the rubber. Channels are then cut into this rubber mould to allow the metal to flow into the cavities. The mould shown is for figures in the author's "Bastion Models" range.*

Above and right: *After dusting with talcum powder the mould is placed on the turntable of the casting machine, a heavy top plate is placed in position, and the lid of the cabinet is lowered. The mould is then spun at high speed while molten metal is poured in through the funnel in the lid. The centrifugal action forces the metal into the cavities to produce a crisp casting of up to a dozen figures attached to a central sprue.*

When buying toy soldiers, shop around first to get an idea of prices. Do not be tempted by overpriced items, however attractive — a cheaper or better example will always turn up.

Most collectors probably have a dream of finding a little out-of-the-way toy shop with shiny red boxes of lead soldiers on the shelves, still at their original prices! Failing this there are several ways of acquiring toy soldiers:

Inform friends and relatives of your interest — they may take pity on you and look in their attics.

Get to know other collectors with whom to swop, buy and sell by joining a society, either the British Model Soldier Society or one of several that exist in the USA.

Get in touch with specialist dealers and let them know your particular requirements; several dealers put out regular lists for buying by post.

Always look in antique and junk shops. Unfortunately, many such dealers believe that any lead figure, whatever the condition, is worth a fortune, but some reasonably-priced items can be found.

There are now regular toy soldier auctions. Prices for the best items can be very high but mixed lots of less-popular figures can still be had fairly cheaply. Remember that people behave rather oddly at auctions, and may bid far higher for a box of soldiers, in the competitive atmosphere, than they would pay over the counter to a dealer. Even if you don't buy, auction views are a very good way to see and become familiar with large quantities of toy soldiers.

CONDITION OF FIGURES

When dealing by post, and describing the condition of toy soldiers, it is useful to have generally accepted terms such as the following:

Mint:

This term should only be used for "factory-fresh" items that have never been removed from their original box.

Excellent:

There should be no obvious sign of any damage to the paintwork, which should have a good original glossy finish to it. Most items optimistically described as "mint" probably belong in this category.

Good:

The figures show some signs of having been played with, but there should be only slight chipping or scratching — preferably not to the head or base. Such figures are still quite acceptable in a collection.

Fair:

These are well played-with figures, but without any damage to the casting, unless stated, and with about 75 per cent of the original paint remaining.

Poor:

Anything worse than fair. This may be acceptable for a rare item that is otherwise almost unobtainable, and in the case of common figures, for stripping and restoring.

TERMINOLOGY

On the following pages certain conventions of terminology have been used throughout. Where appropriate, the size of the figure is indicated in millimetres, this being the accepted practice among toy soldier collectors, but an equivalent in inches is given in all cases. The "size" refers to the height of a standing man without headgear; a mounted figure of the same nominal size is taller.

The manufacturer's original set title has been given where possible, together with the original set number, and is indicated by capital letters. For example: "Belgian Infantry, Review Order; set 189". Such sets normally contained a number of figures, and where possible these are represented on the page by one example of each type — normally an officer and man.

English parade-drill terms have been employed throughout. This may be confusing for American readers, for whom some terms have different meanings. The following American equivalents should be borne in mind when reading the captions: "Slope arms" is known as "shoulder arms" in the USA, while the British "shoulder arms", now obsolete in America, was known as "support arms". The US term for "at ease" is "parade rest".

The earliest toy soldiers produced commercially in any quantity were "flats", first made by the tinsmiths of Nuremberg from the 1730s onwards. The earliest identifiable maker was Johann Gottfried Hilpert, who by the 1770s was making miniatures of the Army of Frederick the Great and some of its opponents. A lot of the early figures were poorly proportioned, and there was no standardization of scale. Ernst Heinrichsen, who set up in business in 1839, produced an enormous range of figures in several sizes, but his most influential achievement was the introduction in 1848 of the standard 30mm (1.8in) figure. The "Nuremberg Scale" soon caught on, and was adopted by many other soldier manufacturers. Although they were also produced in other countries, "flats" have always found most favour in Germany, where they have remained popular to this day. In 1925 Aloys Ochel of Kiel brought out their "Kilia" and "Oki" ranges, aimed at the serious collector as much as at the toy trade. Flats are still being designed and produced, but they are usually sold as unpainted castings to be finished by the purchaser — sometimes to a superb standard of realism.

1-13 French Revolutionary troops of 1796; by Heinrichsen, 1870s. Note both the vigorous action poses of (1-5) and the casual stance of (7-10). In contrast the wounded figure (6) is rather naïvely portrayed. Items (11-13) are mounted officers. The kneeling firing infantryman (5) has a blob of lead at the muzzle of his musket to represent smoke.

14-16 Prussian cavalry of 1813; by Heinrichsen, 1870s. (14-15) show both sides of the same pose, and (16) is a trumpeter.

17 French horse artilleryman; by Heinrichsen, 1860s. This is from the "Sham Fight" set (see *inset*).

18-30 French foot guards, 1840s uniform; by Heinrichsen, c1860. (18-20) are foot guards marching at the shoulder arms. (21-22) are pioneers with axes, wearing their traditional beards and long aprons. (23-29) are bandsmen, including some playing interesting early brass instruments (23-24).

(30) is a mounted guards officer.

31-34 French hussars, 1860s period; by Heinrichsen, 1860s. From the "Sham Fight" set (see *inset*).

35-37 Chasseurs à Cheval of the late 1840s; by Heinrichsen, c1870.

38-48 Scottish Highlanders; by Heinrichsen; c1870. The label on the box lid (see *inset*) identifies them as "Ecossais Montagnards" thus confusing Highlanders with mountain troops. Accordingly they are equipped with mountain artillery pieces carried on mules. They wear rather brief kilts, also spartanly worn by the mounted officer! (41) and (47) show two views of the foot officer; the standard bearer (45) appears to be carrying an Austrian flag.

49-62 The Abyssinian Expedition of 1868; by Heinrichsen, c1870. The

63 64 65 66 67 68 69 70 71 72 73

74 75 76 77 78 79 80 81 82

83 84 85

86 87 88 89 90 91

92 93 94 95 96

97 98 99

infantrymen carry their rifles in three different positions, each shown from either side at (51-53) and (55-57). Three sappers with slung rifles carry an axe, pickaxe and shovel (58-60). Note the officer (50) puffing on a cigar. While all ranks wear the Havelock — a Foreign Legion style cap — an alternative drummer (49) has a sun helmet.

63-70 Austrian infantry of 1680-1700; from the ''Kilia'' range of Aloys Ochel, c1930. These figures capture rather well the late 17th-century uniforms. A more accurate semi-matt paint finish is used, but to the collector this does not have the charm of the glowing semi-translucent colours of the earlier figures.

71-73 Bavarian infantry of the 1830s.

These attractive 48mm (1.9in) figures were produced in Bavaria in the 1960s, from old moulds — demonstrating something of the difficulty involved in trying to date such figures accurately.

74-85 Richard the Lionheart, 1190; by Heinrichsen, c1930. A splendidly colourful set of a battle between Crusaders (77-85) and Saracens (74-76). Note particularly the Crusader with a captured Saracen (78), and the Crusader assisting a comrade (83).

86-91 British rocket battery, 1880; by Heinrichsen, c1930. These notoriously unreliable weapons, introduced by Congreve during the Napoleonic Wars, were still being used (with modifications) in the British Army until the 1890s. The officer (89) and crew are

Inset (above): *Heinrichsen boxes. The large paper-covered wooden box has a sliding lid with a print of a battle scene entitled ''The Sham Fight''. It contains artillery, consisting of fully three-dimensional limbers and cannons pulled by flat horses — see (17) — and hussars as illustrated at (51-54). The split pine boxes on the right are typical of the packaging used for flats in the 18th and 19th centuries. The right-hand box is labelled ''Extra fine tin composition figures — silver prize medal''. The medal is illustrated, showing the head of King Ludwig I of Bavaria. The number of pieces is handwritten, as is the title ''The Abyssinian Expedition'' — the latter in German, French and English. At the bottom of the label is printed ''E. Heinrichsen in Nürnberg''. The label on the other box is similar but shows a gold prize medal with the head of Ludwig II, and the handwritten title ''Ecossais Montagnards''.*

shown in a variety of relaxed poses; the man in shirt sleeves firing the rocket (90) is sometimes painted wearing a scarlet jacket.

92-99 British infantry and Gatling gun, Zulu War, 1879; by Heinrichsen, c1930. Note the traditional feature of the smoke

from the rifles of the two firing figures (96 and 98). The good variety of poses includes two different infantrymen kneeling with fixed bayonets (94 and 99). The sailor crew for the Gatling gun have been given red jackets, as though they were infantry.

"Semi-flat" Figures and Home-cast Moulds

1   2   3   4   5   6   7

27

8

9   10   11   12   13   14

39

15   16   17   18

49

19   20   21   22

23   24   25   26

56

Semi-flats, or semi-solids (*halb massif* in German) are thicker than flats, giving a rounded appearance when viewed from the side. They are rather looked down on by most collectors, and indeed at their worst they can be very crude and uninspired. This is not helped by the fact that many semi-flat moulds were sold for home casting in the 1900s by firms such as Gebrüder Schneider of Leipzig. They were very popular in the USA, where the moulds themselves are collected. The result has been that some very poorly cast semi-flats have found their way on to the market; the dating of the figures has also been made difficult. Despite this there are many exceptions, with a charm

and character of their own, combining the pictorial quality of the flat with a pleasing solidity.

1-7 Austrian cavalry bivouac; *c*1900. Some of the attractive figures from a set currently produced by Kober of Vienna from old moulds by Wollner. A cavalryman in shirtsleeves (1) grooms his horse; (2-4) are dragoons, while (6-7) are hussars.
8 British officer surprised by Zulus. This imaginative piece is by an unknown German maker, *c*1890.
9-14 Austrian artillery, 1880s; by Kober. These Austrian gunners in their distinctive brown tunics serve a fully three-dimensional artillery piece in an attractive group cast from old Wollner moulds. Austrian cannon were

Inset (above) *Old metal home-cast moulds, of designs originally produced by Gebrüder Schneider of Leipzig, together with finished and painted examples of the figures they produce. In the foreground are the British officer, infantryman and Highlander (62-64), and behind are the advancing and marching sailors and the naval officer (50-52).*

traditionally painted yellow.
15-18 Austrian Army field hospital, *c*1900; by Kober. Some of the charming figures from a set produced by Kober from Wollner moulds: (15) a surgeon bandaging the head of a soldier supported by an orderly; (16) a nurse of possibly later design — judging by her raised hemline; (17) an

orderly bandaging a soldier's leg, assisted by a nurse; and (18) two orderlies carrying a wounded man without using a stretcher.
19-26 German sailors, *c*1900; by Schweizer. This German family firm was founded by Adam Schweizer in 1796, and still produces a range of flats and semi-flats in varying sizes, of both military and civilian subjects. (19) depicts a German sailor catching up on the news while leaning against a palm tree and puffing on his pipe. In a smaller scale, (20-26) show a German naval officer supervising sailors going about their tasks and raising the ensign, while other relax.
27-30 The French firm of Mignot, better known for its 54mm (2.12in) solids, also produced an

28 29 30 31 32 33 34 35 36 37 38

40 41 42 43 44 45 46 47 48

50 51 52 53 54 55

57 58 59 60 61 62 63 64

attractive and distinctive range of 40mm (1.57in) semi-flat (*demi ronde bosse*) figures, often available in multi-tiered display boxes including buildings, trees and accessories. These are "Turcos" — French Algerian troops of c1900.

31-38 Allied troops of 1914 by Mignot: (31) French line infantryman marching, parade dress. (32) French line infantryman charging in greatcoat. (33) Belgian infantryman standing firing. (34) Belgian infantryman marching. (35) Russian infantryman marching, parade dress. (36) Russian infantryman advancing in greatcoat. (37-38) British infantry advancing and standing firing. The least satisfactory of an

otherwise good series, the British "Tommies" are in fact Japanese infantry originally designed to oppose (35-36) in a Russo-Japanese war setting, but hurriedly turned out in khaki for World War I. Mignot have never been at their best when portraying British troops!

39-43 French infantry, Franco-Prussian War; by an unknown German maker, c1880. Virtually the same figures were produced in dark blue with German *picklehaubes* (spiked helmets) as Prussians, or in scarlet tunics as British infantry.

44-48 Prussian infantry in action; cast from Schneider moulds of the 1900s. These figures are still being produced commercially on a small scale in England, packed

in cartons and drums marked "Victorian Toy Soldiers".

49 A Prussian bandsman from a Schneider mould, painted as a British soldier.

50-52 German sailors; from an old Schneider mould, recently home-cast and painted (see *inset*).

53-54 A Prussian artilleryman on a draught horse, and an ornate field gun; cast from Schneider moulds by the same firm as (44-48).

55 A small-scale khaki British infantryman of 1914, from a Schneider mould.

56 18th-century infantryman advancing; from a range designed by Holger Eriksson and cast from a modern "Prince August" rubber home-cast mould.

57 A steel-helmeted Swedish cavalryman, designed by Holger

Eriksson and cast from a "Prince August" mould of the 1970s.

58-59 A very basic Soviet soldier at attention with slung sub-machine gun (58), and a trumpeter from a small range of bandsmen (59), made in the USSR in the 1960s.

60-61 Prussian infantry standing and kneeling firing; from a home-cast rubber mould in the "Zinn Brigade" range by Schildkrot. These figures are almost fully round. Home-cast moulds are popular in Germany and available in most large toy shops today. Sadly, the Zinn Brigade range seems to have been discontinued.

62-64 British infantryman and officer, from the Zulu War period, and a Highlander in full dress; commercially produced from a Schneider mould (see *inset*).

23

Solid Figures by Lucotte, France

1 2 3 4 5 6 7

8 9 10

11 12 13 14 15 16 17

While the Germans were producing flat figures in tin the French were developing the fully round solid figure in lead. The earliest known firm, Lucotte, is said to have been founded at about the time of the French Revolution in 1789. Their later amalgamation with C.B.G. Mignot gives the latter firm the distinction of being the oldest toy soldier maker in continuous existence. The bulk of Lucotte's production was devoted to the French Army of the Revolutionary and the First Empire periods. The figures are of excellent quality and have great style; of almost model standard, rather than toys, they must have been expensive playthings. Some fine examples can be seen in museums, and in collections

such as that of the Duke of Marlborough which is on show at Blenheim Palace.
It is difficult to put a date earlier than the 1860s on most of these pieces. Various dates have been put forward for Lucotte's amalgamation with C.B.G. Mignot, but it can be said that soldiers were being produced in the distinctive Lucotte style until after World War I.
Lucotte figures have a longer stride and a lighter step than those by Mignot. They have plug-in heads, and whereas Mignot arms are bent into position those of Lucotte figures are cast separately and fitted over lugs at the shoulder to be soldered in position. The cavalry horses are more elegant than those of

Mignot, with long tails, and the movable reins are applied separately and held in place by pieces of wire. The saddles are removable and have stirrups, although they usually hang too low for the riders' feet to engage in them. Some Lucotte bases are marked with an Imperial Bee flanked by the letters ''LC''.
From time to time Mignot, who hold Lucotte moulds amongst their vast collection, re-issue such items as Napoleon and his staff or a set of cavalry kettle-drummers — at a high price.
Some of the items in Mignot's personality range are of Lucotte origin, such as Marshal Foch (22). For a direct comparison between Lucotte and Mignot figures see the illustration on *page 9*.

1-7 Musicians from the band of the Imperial Guard. Note that two different figures are used — (1, 5, 6), and (2-4). The musicians are: (1) bass drummer; (2) clarinettist; (3) glockenspiel player; (4) clarinettist; (5) serpent player (this was a cumbersome instrument of wood bound in leather); (6) trombone player. The splendid tall figure in the extravagantly plumed hat and red boots (7), missing most of his staff in this example, is in fact a portrait figure of Drum Major Senot who served with the band of the Imperial Guard throughout the Napoleonic period.
8 Napoleonic lancer of the Vistula Legion. Note that this excellent figure of a Polish lancer and all the following Lucotte cavalry have separate saddles and also

18 **19** **20**

21 **22** **23**

24 **25** **26** **27** **28** **29** **30**

feature separate movable reins.

9 Trooper of the 5th Hussars. He wears a separately cast pelisse (fur-trimmed jacket) hanging from the left shoulder.

10 Officer of the 5th Hussars. He is dressed similarly to the trooper, but correctly wears a fur busby rather than a shako and has a different pattern saddle cloth.

11 British infantryman, Waterloo period. Note the particularly jaunty step of this and some of the other figures.

12 A British infantry drummer in "reverse" colours: his jacket is in green-facing colour rather than red, and trimmed with distinctive "drummer's lace".

13 French line infantryman of the Napoleonic period, marching at the slope.

14 French infantryman, in the white uniform of 1806. This uses the same body casting as (13) but with a taller plumed shako.

15 French infantryman, in white uniform, at the present arms.

16 Standard-bearer of the Flanqueurs of the Imperial Guard, 1812-14.

17 Flanqueur, marching at the shoulder arms.

18-22 A series of mounted personality figures of World War I. Note that the next five models all have the same horse and rider casting; apart from the painting only the portrait head and sometimes the saddlery varies. (18) King George V in the World War I khaki service dress of a general officer. (19) General Cadorna, Commander-in-Chief of

the Italian Army, in pre-war style uniform. (20) King Peter of Serbia. (21) General John Pershing, Commander of the First US Army, in campaign hat. (22) Marshal Foch; interestingly, this is a figure currently available from C.B.G. Mignot in their personality range, but unlike most of the series it is entirely Lucotte in design, the base of the horse being marked with an Imperial Bee flanked by the letters LC.

23 Indian Army cavalry trooper, in khaki World War I uniform.

24 Indian Army sepoy, in World War I khaki, marching at the slope. See (40) *page 28* for the Mignot sepoy.

25 Chasseur Alpin (or mountain light infantryman), standing firing. This casting, rather shorter than most Lucotte figures, was also issued

in khaki with a steel helmet as a British Tommy.

26 Chasseur Alpin, kneeling firing. See (26-27) *page 29* for Mignot Chasseurs Alpin.

27 French infantryman, prone firing, in "Adrian" helmet and horizon blue greatcoat. Compare with the similar Mignot figure shown at (41) *page 26*.

28 French standard-bearer, in horizon blue tunic. The Mignot equivalent to this figure is shown at (4) *page 26*.

29 French infantry bugler, in "Adrian" pattern helmet and horizon blue greatcoat. Note the separately applied *fouragerre* or lanyard on the left shoulder.

30 French infantryman, in horizon blue uniform, depicted at the order arms position.

The firm of C.B.G. Mignot of Paris, with a lineage dating back via takeovers and their absorption of Lucotte to the period of the French Revolution, can claim to be the oldest toy soldier maker still in existence. C.B.G. stands for Cuperly, Blondel and Gerbeau — three early 19th-century makers who amalgamated and were taken over by Mignot. A large part of the Mignot range depicts Napoleonic troops, but it has also covered the spectrum from Ancient Greeks, Romans, Gauls and Huns to the Israeli Army of the 1950s. The 54mm (2.12in) solid range of figures is the most important, but Mignot also made 40mm (1.57in) semi-flats — see (27-38) page 23 — some large hollow-casts, aluminium figures,

and second-grade 54mm (2.12in) hollow-casts, as well as an extensive range of flats which are still produced. Hand-cast in bronze moulds, their 54mm (2.12in) solid figures emerge from the mould headless and with arms outspread. After cleaning the casting a suitable head is plugged in, and the arms are "animated" or bent into position to receive a weapon or musical instrument which is soldered on. The figures are then painted. In the past, infantry were issued in sets of 12, with an officer, standard bearer and drummer or bugler. Cavalry were in boxes of six. Cavalry are now five to a box, and infantry are in sets of 12 or eight figures — still in shiny red boxes. Infantry are also sold in

clear plastic-fronted boxes of four. Figures dating from the 1900s have dark green bases and a particularly good-quality paint finish, and contemporary troops carry the Chassepot rifle which has a more prominent sword bayonet than the later Lebel rifle. In the 1930s a very light sand colour was used for bases, and the facial detail which is such a feature of Mignot soldiers was not always so well painted. In the 1970s a rather "thin" full-gloss painting was adopted, and the bases were painted very dark brown. From about 1979 a semi-matt or satin finish painting has been used. Current figures have "C.B.G. Made in France" or just "Made in France" impressed into the base.

1 Monaco Carabinier at attention; white summer uniform.
2 Gun team with 75mm gun. This version with artillerymen in dark blue was produced in the 1970s.
3 French Army De Dion Bouton staff car, with driver, officer in kepi and NCO in greatcoat holding a map. This is a recent revival of a c1905 item.
4 French World War I standard bearer, in horizon blue uniform.
5 Marshal Joffre. This personality figure, produced c1930, is not just a head change, as he has the authentic portly figure!
6 A personality figure of Marshal Lyautey, produced c1980 in gloss finish. Strangely this figure uses the same body casting as the Hindou at (40) page 28.
7 A personality figure of Lyautey as

Governor-General of Morocco, in an Arab cloak.

8 Officer of hussars, in 1900s full dress, in current production.

9 Chasseur à Cheval, produced c1930, in 1915 horizon blue.

10 St Cyr cadet, from the mounted squadron in current production.

11 Officer of Dragons, 1900, in cloak; in current production.

12-15 Artillerymen in horizon blue, currently available.

16 Fortress cannon, an impressive item, recently discontinued.

17 World War I motor truck, of recent production.

18-29 The well-known Hommes de Corvée, or fatigue party. Note that these are infantryman — not engineers as they are sometimes incorrectly described. Apart from the NCO (18) they all use the same casting with an undress cap and a typically French canvas smock. Among the items carried are a side of bacon (22) and a broom with real twigs (24). This is a 1970s gloss-paint production. These figures have appeared with a number of different paint finishes and heads — see (30).

30 British soldier in fatigue dress with shovel.

31-33 British artillery of the 1900s, produced c1905. This interesting piece uses the same gun team as (2), including the famous French ''75'' gun, but with mounted artillerymen in khaki foreign service helmets as worn in the South African War. The gunners seated on the limber and the two marching figures (32 and 33) wear the peaked caps introduced into the British Army in 1905.

34 Mounted British artillery officer, to accompany the gun team. Based on the same casting as (8), but in khaki with a foreign service helmet, he has inappropriate frogging cast on his tunic.

35 Italian lancer, World War I.

36 Italian dragoon, World War I.

37 French line infantryman advancing, 1914.

38 French horizon blue infantryman, in greatcoat, kneeling firing; of recent manufacture.

39 French horizon blue infantryman advancing; recent manufacture. This is the same figure as (37) but with a steel helmet.

40 French horizon blue infantryman in greatcoat, standing firing.

41 French horizon blue infantryman in greatcoat, prone firing.

42 French horizon blue infantryman, standing firing; unusually in a tunic rather than a greatcoat.

43 French horizon blue machine-gunner; of recent manufacture.

44 French Foreign Legionnaire, advancing; recently re-issued.

45 US infantryman, standing firing, 1917.

46 US infantryman, advancing.

47 Chasseur Alpin ski trooper; a recent re-issue, also available in dark blue uniform.

48 French horizon blue despatch rider, on what is a virtually flat motorcycle; 1970s.

49 Monaco cannon; to accompany the Monaco Carabiniers.

50 Mountain gun. Despite its list description, this strange looking weapon is quite different from the Mignot mountain battery gun.

Solid and Hollow-cast Figures by Mignot, France

1 15th-century halberdier. This attractive figure also comes in red, green and white costume, and with a different pole arm.

2 Infantry of Francis I, 16th century.

3 Pikeman of Henri IV, 17th century.

4 Musketeer of Henri IV. This is the same body casting as (3) but with a soft felt hat and an arquebus.

5 Musketeer of Louis XIII, 17th century.

6 Swiss Guard of Louis XIV, armed with a halberd; the sword is missing. The Swiss were distinguished by red coats.

7 Line infantryman of Louis XIV, the Champagne Regiment, 1670. This is the same as (6) but with the white coat of the line infantry.

8 Line infantryman of Louis XV, the Regiment de Tourraine, 1740. The coat now has turnbacks, the hair is powdered and the hat is definitely a tricorn.

9 Grenadier Guard of Louis XV. This casting is the same as (8).

10 French Guards of Louis XVI, 1789. The same body casting as (9) but with a tall bearskin cap.

11 8th Bavarian Regiment, 1812. Note the distinctive helmet. This example is in 1970s gloss finish.

12 Russian grenadier, 1807.

13 French Marine of the Guard, 1812.

14 British infantry drummer, 1812.

15 British infantryman, 1812.

16 French line infantry standard-bearer, 1860. This officer in a frock coat carries a finely detailed standard topped with an eagle.

17 French line infantryman, 1860s. Unlike the officer, this private wears a short tunic over baggy trousers and white spats.

18-19 French line infantry, 1900s. These are unusual second-grade figures. Unlike (20) the pack is cast integrally. The arms are soldered on, and while the torso is fully round the legs are semi-flat.

20 French line infantry in full dress tunic, 1914. This example is in 1980s semi-matt finish.

21-22 Officer and man, French line infantry, in greatcoats, 1914. Note that the officer does not have the edges of his coat turned back.

23-24 Officer and man, Chasseurs à Pied; produced c1900. Note that unlike later versions this officer has a full epaulette on the left shoulder, and a fringeless crescent on the right. This indicates a lieutenant, which is in accord with the two rings on his sleeve. The private wears the double-breasted tunic which was replaced in the French Army by a single-breasted tunic in 1889.

25 Dismounted Cuirassier officer, 1914. The troopers use the same casting but carry drawn swords. A 1970s example in gloss finish.

26-27 Officer and man of the Chasseurs Alpins. These French mountain troops are also available in white uniforms. Note that the officer has a walking stick, and that the men carry them on their packs (27). This is a 1970s gloss painting.

28-29 Officer and man, Gardes de Paris, or Republican Guards. Note that the officer body casting is the same as that used for infantry and Chasseurs, but with a separately applied aiguillette. The

men use a special casting with a long stride similar to (24), without epaulettes and with cast-on aiguillette detail. Unusually both figures are marked ''C.B.G. Paris'' in raised letters on the tops of their bases.

30 Cadet, Ecole Polytechnique. A cadet from the military academy where French artillery and engineer officers are trained.

31-32 Officer and Porte-Fanion, Foreign Legion. These figures wear the khaki uniform of the 1920s. Instead of a standard bearer the set contains an NCO with a company flag on his rifle.

33 French Army medical orderly, in a double-breasted jacket with a backpack marked with a red cross. The French Army changed from horizon blue to khaki

uniforms in the mid-1930s.

34 French infantryman; from the fatigue party shown on *page 27*, in undress cap and smock. This example is in 1970s gloss paint.

35-36 Officer and man, French Colonial infantry, 1880. These are 1980s re-issues. Note the Chassepot rifle and sword bayonet, rather than the Lebel of most of the other figures. This body casting is used as the basis for many figures, including (32), (37), (41) and (45-48).

37 Senegalese Tirailleur, of 1914.

38 Algerian Tirailleur, or ''Turco'', as they were known, of 1914.

39 Zouave, of 1914.

40 Indian Army sepoy, or ''Hindou'' as Mignot called him.

41 Egyptian Army infantryman.

42 Greek Evzone. The casting for

this was also used for the officer.

43 The Italian Bersaglieri. This figure uses a special Italian Army casting with shoulder wings, and turned-back tunic skirts to reveal an ammunition pouch worn beneath. The figure wears the well-known broad-brimmed hat with cock's-feather plume.

44 Monaco Carabinieri, marching in summer uniform. The guards of this tiny principality are also produced in blue winter dress. The body casting used is that of the 1860s officer (16).

45 Portuguese infantryman, in the horizon blue uniform that was adopted during World War I.

46 Serbian infantryman, in the uniform of the 1900s.

47 Siamese Guard, 1900. This unusual figure is from one of six

sets of Siamese Guards and infantry listed in the 1900s.

48 US infantryman, 1917. Although using one of the standard body castings, this ''doughboy'' in campaign hat has the correct US 1910-pattern backpack.

49 A ''Sakaleve'', or native of Madagascar. This figure was also produced armed with a spear.

50 Serbian infantryman in khaki, kneeling firing.

51 French naval officer, 1914. This example is in 1970s gloss finish. An earlier version had a head with a small-crowned cap and mutton-chop whiskers.

52 A second-grade sailor similar in appearance to the first-grade type, but hollow-cast.

53 A second-grade hollow-cast horizon blue French infantryman.

Solid Figures by Heyde, Germany

Although solid (and semi-solid) figures had been produced sporadically in Germany since the 18th century, the home market was dominated by the flat tin soldier. In the early 1870s, however, perhaps influenced by the success of the excellent solid figures produced by Lucotte and Mignot, Georg Heyde of Dresden started producing solid lead soldiers on a regular basis. Despite the charm of his figures he never really threatened the position of the ''flat'' in his own country, and had his greatest success with exports to countries such as Britain and the USA. Heyde produced figures in a bewildering variety of styles and scales — seven main infantry sizes from 43-120mm (1.7-4.7in),

the most numerous being the 43mm (1.7in) followed by the 52mm (2in) sizes. As with Mignot figures a fairly small number of different malleable soft lead bodies and plug-in heads with suitable paint finishes were able to represent almost any uniform or pose desired, but whatever the army represented, the figure retained a ''Germanic'' look. Heyde's smaller-scale soldiers were often lumpy, ill-proportioned little things, but his great achievement was in the imaginative uses to which he put them. Ordinary marching and firing figures were certainly produced, but what Heyde is most noted for are great ceremonial parades, and working parties going about their chores,

launching observation balloons, or following more tranquil occupations in a bivouac.

1 Scottish piper at attention. A good figure of a Gordon Highlander, only marred by a rather odd-shaped glengarry. This is to 52mm (2in) scale, the remainder of the figures shown — except (26) — being in the smaller 43mm (1.7in) size.
2 British Guardsman at attention.
3 Guards colour bearer, with the usual rather strange interpretation of the Union Flag.
4 Guards side drummer, with drummer's lace, but also a German-style backpack.
5 Marching Guards officer.
6 Guardsman, marching with his rifle at the slope.

7 Guards officer, in action with drawn sword.
8 Guardsman, standing firing.
9 Guardsman, kneeling firing.
10-18 German Navy working party, comprising: (10) sailor walking empty-handed; (11) sailor scrubbing the deck with a broom; (12) sailor with a coil of rope over his arm; (13) sailor coiling a rope on the deck; (14) sailor carrying a bucket; (15) sailor carrying a barrel; (16) sailor carrying a box on his shoulder; (17) sailor emptying a bucket; (18) sailor with a broom over his arm.
19 British line infantryman, marching with fixed bayonet in a white foreign service helmet.
20 British line infantry colour bearer, in spiked helmet.
21 British line infantryman, in foreign

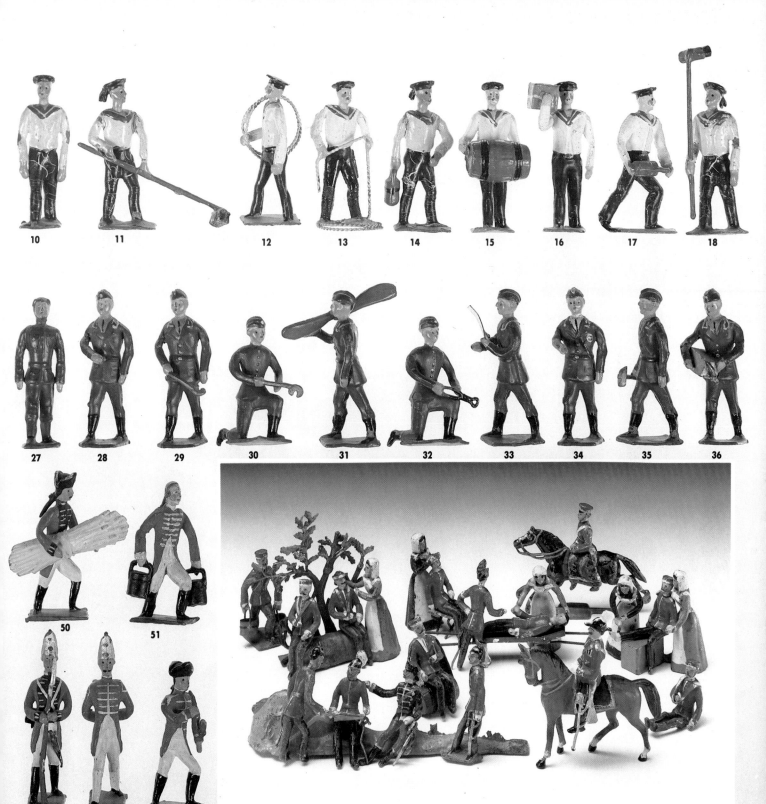

Inset (above): *In the foreground Lord Kitchener rides up to discuss the progress of the battle with his officers of, from left to right, infantry, dragoons, hussars and lancers. Behind them nurses care for the wounded under the supervision of a medical officer, while an orderly brings water. In the background a FANY nurse gallops off, side-saddle, to rescue a wounded soldier from the battlefield. In 1907 the First Aid Nursing Yeomanry (FANY) was formed of women to be trained in first aid and riding. Only Heyde depicted them in their intended role — no British manufacturer did. In fact the FANY personnel served as ambulance drivers during World War I.*

service helmet, standing firing.

22-23 Variations of (19).

24 Line infantryman, marching at the slope in spiked helmet.

25 Line infantry officer, in action with drawn sword.

26 British Army cyclist, in scarlet jacket and glengarry; 52mm (2in) size. Heyde produced at least two quite distinct patterns of bicycle.

27-36 Luftwaffe pilot and ground crew. The German air force or Luftwaffe was formed in 1935. The figures here are: (27) pilot, using US "doughboy" body with a flying-helmet head; (28) airman walking empty-handed; (29) airman walking with spanner; (30) airman kneeling with spanner; (31) airman carrying a propeller; (32) airman kneeling with pliers; (33) airman carrying papers; (34)

Luftwaffe officer — this uses the same casting as the men, but with a "Sam Browne" cross-belt painted in, a white shirt, and a silver pilot badge; (35) airman carrying a large hammer; (36) airman emptying a petrol can.

37-49 British World War I working party, comprising: (37) British officer — very much a Prussian figure in British uniform; (38) British soldier with slung rifle holding the lead of a guard dog; (39) British soldier carrying a sandbag on his shoulder — this figure and (41-42, 44-45) use a US Army "doughboy" casting; (40) British soldier patrolling with rifle at the ready; (41-42) two soldiers carrying spools of telephone cable; (43) an empty-handed figure which probably

carried a shovel originally; (44) soldier carrying two buckets; (45) soldier carrying a nicely-modelled bow-saw; (46) soldier with a pick-axe; (47) soldier kneeling to unleash a guard dog; (48) soldier trudging along with rifle at the slope; (49) a very German-looking British officer in a soft peaked cap, with a walking stick.

50-54 American War of

Independence British Army bivouac. Some individual figures from the scene featured on the endpapers of this book: (50) infantryman carrying a bale of hay; (51) bare-headed soldier carrying buckets; (52) grenadier on guard duty; (53) grenadier off duty walking with his hands behind his back; (54) off-duty infantryman smoking a pipe.

Solid Figures by Heyde, Germany

1-15 The following are a selection from the many figures in Heyde's "Delhi Durbar" set.

1 Indian lancer, from a detachment of Bengal Lancers which were accompanied by a mounted band.

2 Indian camel-mounted kettle-drummer, with hanging trappings. The camel is rather small and semi-flat compared with (4).

3 Trumpeter, from what is intended to be a British cavalry band.

4 A camel lancer, from one of the state forces. The camel, with rather strange ears, is much larger than (2), has separate reins and is free-standing. The full set contained about a dozen of these figures, headed by a rajah with a young prince seated in front of him, both astride a camel with a red saddle cloth.

5 Heyde had a fondness for elephants — this roaring beast also turns up in other sets. Here he is furnished with rich colourful trappings and an ornate howdah, containing a maharajah and his fan bearer.

6 This remarkable figure is of a warrior with sword and shield mounted on stilts. Apparently the more impoverished states, which could not afford elephants themselves, made use of stilt men to attack warriors on elephants!

7 A British officer of a Madras cavalry regiment.

8 This bare-back rider who appears to be showing off probably had the same function as the stilt man at (6), being trained to attack elephant-borne troops. Close examination of this figure reveals a clever re-use by Heyde of a kilted Scottish Highlander casting: concealed under the paint of his "kaftan" is a Highland doublet, kilt and sporran!

9 An Indian retainer carrying a long-handled sunshade, to walk alongside a mounted dignitary.

10 King George V on horseback, in general's uniform and wearing a plumed white foreign service helmet. In the set he is accompanied by a cluster of assorted generals and dignitaries.

11 Indian cavalryman, wearing antiquated armour: probably a soldier from Jammu and Kashmir, who had some armoured cavalry.

12 Indian cavalryman, in turban and European style uniform — possibly an artilleryman.

13 An Indian retainer armed with a spear and a round shield.

14 An Indian retainer playing a pipe, from a band of native musicians.

15 British line infantryman, in foreign service helmet, from a detachment included in this set.

16-38 "The Triumph of Germanicus". This splendid set by Heyde came in three different versions, one of which contained 60 items. The set depicted the triumphal return to Rome of Germanicus, nephew of the Emperor Tiberius, in AD17 following his victories in Germany over the tribes led by Hermann, and the recovery of the "eagles" of the legions massacred in the Battle of the Teutoberger Forest. A splendid elephant was also included in the set, but unlike that in the Durbar set this animal was depicted walking with its trunk

down, carrying an ornate throne.

16 An elegant two-horse chariot driven by a helmeted charioteer holding a cavalry standard.

17 Germanicus on his triumphal car pulled by four horses. Crowned with a laurel wreath and with a sceptre in his hand the hero sits enthroned, accompanied by a driver and a standard bearer.

18 A cavalry trumpeter on a rather fine long-tailed horse which was probably also used with medieval figures. Heyde seems to have had an enormous range of different horses. With some manufacturers the limited range of horse types can be an aid to identification, but not so with Heyde.

19 A marching soldier playing a long trumpet or "bucina".

20-24 Legionaries; note that there

are two different body castings and two types of spear. The rectangular and hexagonal shields are cast, while the circular ones are made of tinplate and usually left in shiny finish; that of (24) has probably been embellished by a former owner.

25 This figure in an animal-skin hood is found with a trumpet like (19) and as such may represent a "loyal" German.

26 A foot soldier bearing a laurel wreath — perhaps to signify a particular victory.

27 Although Roman citizens are included in the set this pair represents the wife and son of the German leader Hermann, who were brought captive to Rome.

28 A Roman lady bystander. Both this female figure and (27) turn up

in many guises and periods of history in Heyde sets.

29 A foot soldier holding an infantry standard — perhaps one of those recovered from the Germans.

30 A cloaked figure bearing a tray of loaves — presumably an offering to the Gods. A similar figure is included in "The Sack of Troy".

31 A soldier with a wolfhound brought from Germany.

32 A bear from the German forest, with its handler.

33-34 Roman cavalrymen.

35 A Roman cavalry officer.

36 A pole topped with a victory wreath and shield to line the processional route.

37 An attractively modelled banner flying from a pole.

38 A column topped by a sacrificial flame. This item is also found in

"The Sack of Troy" set.

39-43 "The Sack of Troy" set contained some of the walls and temples of Troy, a selection of Greek and Trojan warriors, Achilles in a chariot like (16) dragging the body of Hector behind him — with a distraught King Priam looking on, and awful scenes of slaughter like those shown here.

39 A Greek warrior with his foot on one fallen Trojan has just felled a second and turns to attack a third.

40 A bare-fisted struggle, apparently between two Trojans.

41 A Greek warrior charges with sword upraised.

42 A Trojan warrior reels back from the onslaught.

43 Another scene of carnage as a Greek fells a Trojan.

1   2   3   4   5   6   14   15   16   17

7   8   9   10   11   27   28

12   13   36   37

Heyde produced an enormous range of solid lead soldiers, and it is easy to attribute all unidentified figures to that maker, but there were many other firms producing similar work.

1-4 Prussian infantry in full parade dress; from a boxed set of the 1890s marked "GZ" for Gebrüder Zerwick, apparently of Vienna, although the label indicates made in Germany. They are: (1) a standard bearer with Prussian colours; (2) an infantryman marching at the slope; (3) a bugler with a bandsman's red plume; (4) an infantry officer.

5-6 Royal Navy whitejacket and marine; probably by the German firm of Spenkuch, c1910.

7-13 The following large-size figures

are by Gebrüder Heinrich, c1900.

7 An excellent Chelsea pensioner.

8 Private of the British West India Regiment.

9 Turkish Army Zouave. This uses the same body casting as (8).

10 Highland piper at attention.

11 Prussian infantryman at attention.

12 Trumpeter, from a mounted Household Cavalry band.

13 An excellent portrait figure of General Sir Redvers Buller V.C., the only error being that his Rifle Brigade uniform has been painted dark blue rather than dark green!

14-26 Brigader-Statuette of Denmark, who started production in 1946, are best known for their range of Danish footguards — see (14). Less well known are their Danish troops in the uniform of the 1900s, very reminiscent of Heyde

— note the stance of (21-24).

14 Marching Guards officer.

15 Marching infantry officer.

16 Infantry bugler.

17 Infantryman marching at the slope.

18-20 Stretcher bearers with wounded infantryman.

21 Infantryman advancing.

22 Infantryman advancing with a Madsen machine-gun.

23 Artilleryman standing with shell.

24 Artilleryman with ram-rod.

25 Kneeling artilleryman, setting the fuse on a shell.

26 Kneeling artilleryman, loading a shell into a gun.

27-45 There have been a surprising number of Spanish lead soldier makers, many of them concentrated in Barcelona. The first known maker was Ortelli,

who came to Barcelona from Italy in 1828. He produced an extensive range of large flats, covering virtually all of the Spanish Army of the period, and many civilian themes as well. Solid 54mm (2.12in) figures appeared in 1897 with the "La Guerra" range of Casanellas. In 1925 the range was taken over by the Capell brothers, but with an increasing proportion of 45mm (1.77in) figures.

The other maker of solids at this time was Eulogio Gonzalez who, under the name "Eulogio", produced figures with a more rugged and sculptural quality than those of the La Guerra range. Cap cords and aiguillettes were applied separately to the figures, and horses and mules had a

18   19   20   21   22   23   24   25   26

29   30   31   32   33   34   35

38   39   40   41

42   43   44   45

zig-zag of wire soldered to their hooves to act as a base.
In 1922 Pedro Palomeque started production in Madrid of an excellent series of 54mm (2.12in) figures. Reminiscent of Mignot in style, the range included contemporary army figures, Romans, medieval troops, 18th-century courtiers, and horse-drawn vehicles. Sadly, Palomeque's factory was destroyed in the Spanish Civil War.
After the Civil War the brothers Sanquez of Madrid produced an interesting range of 50mm (2in) figures. The infantry had fully round torsos and movable arms, but semi-flat legs, which stylistically worked quite well. Plug-in heads made a large range possible from a relatively small

variety of body castings. They also made some delightful 30mm (1.2in) "sand table" or war game figures (see *page 16*). When Sanquez ceased production in 1946, their designs were taken over by other makers, especially Pech Hermanos of Barcelona who produced them in quantity but in an inferior quality.
Finally in the 1940s one Fernandez Aira, trading from Madrid under the name "Multicolor", produced an extensive range of 45mm (1.77in) solid lead figures. These were packaged in small cartons resembling books, each containing one cavalryman or two infantry, entitled "The Military History of Spain — in Lead Soldiers" (see *page 16*).

27-29 Mounted officer, gunner and ammunition mule, from a 45mm (1.77in) La Guerra mountain battery, 1920s. The set contained three more mules which carried the barrel, trail and wheels of a small mountain howitzer.
30 Hussar de Pavia in undress peaked cap, by Palomeque, to 54mm (2.12in) scale. The prominent nose and style of painting the eyebrow are typical of Palomeque.
31 Spanish infantryman in service dress with steel helmet, designed by Sanquez but here produced by Pech Hermanos.
32 Guardia Civil in gala dress, designed and produced by Pech Hermanos in the Sanquez style.
33 Spanish Army medical orderly, from a 54mm (2.12in) scale

stretcher party set by La Guerra.
34 Spanish Moroccan soldier, by La Guerra.
35 Spanish infantryman in greatcoat. A characteristics Sanquez design, which with different plug-in heads was used for a number of figures. This example was cast by Pech Hermanos, in zinc alloy.
36-45 A selection from the "Multicolor" Military History of Spain series: (36) an Ancient warrior; (37) a Roman soldier; (38) a 13th-century knight; (39) a 16th-century Spanish soldier with arquebus; (40) infantry, Regiment de Sevilla, 1745; (41) line infantry, Regiment Isabelinos, 1839; (42) a Hussar de Pavia, 1900; (43) an infantryman in gala dress 1918; (44) an airman, 1940s; (45) a marine, 1940s.

Compared with other toy soldier makers Britains made quite a feature of military bands. These are very popular with collectors.

1 Band of the Coldstream Guards; set 37. This version was produced from 1895-1910, but a Coldstream Guard band remained in the catalogue until 1959. The figures have unmarked oval bases, gaiters and ''slotted arms'' — the instrument arms are fitted into slots in the body and held rigidly in position by solder. This was always a 21-piece set; the band shown is missing one trombone. The drum major's mace is cast integrally, but on later bands the mace is longer and cast separately, being riveted on which allows some movement.

The bombardon (extreme left, third row of musicians) was a feature of the early bands, being replaced in 1910 by a bass horn. From 1933 one euphonium and one trumpet were deleted and replaced by a tenor horn and a double bass horn.

2 Band of the Royal Scots Greys; set 1721. This excellent 12-piece band (one of the trumpeters had gone on sick parade when the photograph was taken) was only available in 1939-40. The seven-piece set 1720 introduced at the same time reappeared post-war and remained available until 1965. It contained the following instruments: kettle drums, cymbals, tuba, clarinet, bassoon, trombone and trumpet. Note that the kettle drummer alone rides a

black horse and has a white ''bearskin'', said to have been presented by Tsar Nicholas II of Russia. All the musicians have red plumes over the tops of their caps, rather than the usual white.

3 Royal Marine bandsmen. Not a complete band, these musicians are from the very popular 12- and 21-piece sets introduced in 1934. The 12-piece set 1291 contained: a drum major, two trombonists, two trumpeters, two euphonium players, one fifer, one cymbalist, two side drummers and a bass drummer. The 21-piece set 1288 had additionally: one tenor horn player, one bass horn player and one double-bass horn player, two clarinettists, one bassoonist, one extra trumpeter and two extra side drummers. Reflecting actual

Royal Marine practice, both bands had more side drummers than other sets. In 1956, for one year only, set 2115: Drums and Bugles of the Royal Marines replaced the 12-piece set. This consisted of a drum major, bass drummer, a cymbalist, three side drummers, a tenor drummer, and five buglers. This does not seem to have been a popular set, as it was replaced the following year (making it very scarce) by a new 12-piece band with plastic drums: set 2153. This band, which lasted only until 1960, contained a drum major, one trombonist, one euphonium player, one clarinettist, one bassoonist, one fifer, one cymbalist, three side drummers, one bass drummer, and a tenor drummer. The gaitered bass

3

4

5

drummer shown is unusual, in that drummers and drum majors in gaiters were given full trousers to match the musician figures very soon after the introduction of the Royal Marine bands in 1934.

4 Band of the Life Guards; set 101. A mounted Life Guard band in state dress was available from 1899, the first version having "slotted arm" musicians. There was also a Horse Guards band: set 103, but this was fairly short-lived. The magnificent gold-laced state dress dates back to the time of Charles II, except for the "jockey cap" which is Victorian. It is really a Royal livery, only worn on state occasions; at other times regimental dress is worn. For the record a state occasion is a parade or ceremony at which

the sovereign (or his or her personal representative) is present, a ceremony celebrating the sovereign's birthday, or a ceremony held in the presence of a member of the Royal Family and which is designated as such. This splendid band, from the 1930s, consists of: one kettle drummer on a piebald horse, two trombonists, one cymbalist, three clarinettists (more usually two clarinettists and one fifer), one bassoonist, two trumpeters, one bass horn player and one euphonium player. In the post-war version re-introduced in 1953 the musicians lost their swords, and the fifer was deleted in favour of a director of music in regimental dress of white plumed helmet and scarlet tunic carrying a baton.

The set was available until 1965.

5 Band of the Line; set 27. The first version (1895-1910) of the first band listed by Britains, with unmarked oval bases and slotted arms, using the same figures as the Coldstream Guards band but with infantry spiked helmets. The composition of the band is: drum major, two euphonium and trombone players, one cymbalist, a bass drummer and side drummer, three trumpeters and a fifer, which was sometimes substituted for a bombardon player. The bandsmen have white facings (collars and cuffs), so they can represent almost any English line regiment of the period which is not a "Royal" regiment. Since 1881 Royal regiments had blue facings while other

regiments had white facings; over the years many regained their cherished original distinctive colours. Set 30, Drums and Bugles of the Line, originally comprised a drum major, bass drummer, two side drummers, and four buglers, and had blue facings, thus representing a Royal regiment. Over the years the set dwindled to five pieces.

From 1910 the bandsmen were slightly taller, with movable arms and square bases. Musicians became straight-trousered soon afterwards, but drum majors, bass drummers and side drummers kept their gaiters until c1935 giving the bands of the intervening period a rather ill-matched look. For later bands, see *pages 82-83*.

Household Cavalry by Britains, UK

Britains' first two sets were 1: The Life Guards and set 2: The Horse Guards of the Household Cavalry. These were the same castings with different painting details.

1 Life Guard of 1837. This is the second-version Life Guard produced in 1897, with fixed arm and tin-strip sword. It is from an unnumbered box of 12 Life Guards issued to celebrate Queen Victoria's Diamond Jubilee (1837-97). Half the figures wear the uniform of 1897, much the same as that worn today, and the others wear this magnificent "Romanesque" helmet and have the white paint of their breeches taken up to waist level.
2 The 1902 version Life Guard, now with a movable arm. Note the

aiguillettes on the chest, discontinued a few years later.
3-4 The very first versions of Britains Life Guards and Horse Guards from 1893. Note the small horse, tin-strip sword and generally "Continental" look. The earliest sets have five figures of the same casting, and the officer is distinguished only by a gold waist sash. These figures are not as uncommon as might be expected, because although replaced in the first-quality sets by 1897, they continued to be sold in simpler packaging in the "X" series for a number of years.
5 Horse Guards officer, on prancing "one-eared" horse, with tin-strip sword and wedge-shaped base, c1894. This impressive figure replaced the trooper with gold

sash initially used to represent an officer in sets 1 and 2. He was also used, with scarlet jacket and red and white plume, in set 3: The 5th Dragoon Guards, and for this purpose the casting included a throat plume dangling from the reins. This was normally snipped off for Household Cavalry.
6 Horse Guards trooper of 1897-1902. This is similar to much later figures but with aiguillettes, a fixed arm holding a tin-strip sword and a "one-eared" horse — for ease of casting there is no indentation between the horse's ears, a feature which Britains corrected on later versions.
7 Life Guard Trumpeter in State Dress. Available in sets 2067, 2085 and as a Picture Pack, this is a much later figure than those

discussed so far, not appearing until 1953. Like many other figures this was inspired by the coronation of Queen Elizabeth II.
8 Life Guards officer on rearing horse; set 1, issued 1946-53. The officer casting (5) was converted to a movable-armed figure in 1902, and then replaced by this casting in 1909. The paint style shows this to be a post-war example, made before 1953 when it was replaced by an officer on a more sedately trotting horse more suitable for a coronation procession. Interestingly, although revived at this date, the Horse Guards officer did not receive the new horse.
9 2nd Life Guards trooper galloping with carbine; set 43, early 1930s. Until 1922, when they

38

4

5

6

10

11

12

17

18

19

20

amalgamated, there had been two regiments of Life Guards. These were most readily identifiable by their sheepskin saddle covers: the 1st's were black, and the 2nd's were white. After the amalgamation white sheepskins were worn. Britains produced the 2nd Life Guards right up to World War II.

10 Horse Guards trooper at the gallop with sword. This figure was only available as part of the squadron of Royal Horse Guards riding with a complete company of Coldstream Guards in a 71-piece Display Set, no. 93. Some unusual figures could be obtained only in the larger sets. This trooper dates from the late 1930s. See also (12).

11 Horse Guards trooper; set 2. He

is mounted on the perfected horse introduced in 1912 which no longer has a carbine on the saddle and now has two ears! His rather thin sword compared with (2) puts him later than 1925, and the fact that Britains have not given him a red collar, which they did in 1935, neatly dates him to around 1930.

12 Horse Guards trooper at the gallop with lance; set 93, c1900. This is the first version with a slightly "Germanic" look; note that because his scabbard is moulded as empty he has in effect lost his sword. See (10).

13 Life Guards Farrier Corporal of Horse, available in set 2067 from 1953-66, and in Picture Pack 1270B from 1954-59. Despite first appearances this figure with a

ceremonial axe is a Life Guard, and is distinguished from a Horse Guard farrier by his black hanging plume and white sheepskin.

14 Life Guard in winter cloak, set 400. This simple, elegant figure first appeared in 1930 and remained in the catalogue until the end of production in 1966. The officer used the same casting with an empty-handed arm, rather than the outstretched sword arm.

15 Life Guards trooper; set 1. This shows the new walking horse with head up, introduced in 1953, as well as the new head with falling plume of the same date.

16 Life Guard foot sentry; set 2029. One of the foot figures from a set comprising two mounted Life Guards at the halt, and four dismounted troopers. The set was

produced from 1949 until the end, but lost one foot sentry in 1960.

17-18 Horse Guards Sentry on Foot, and Horse Guards Trooper at the Halt; Picture Packs 1340B and 1336B. Oddly, unlike the Life Guards these figures were never combined in a set, but were only available individually in 1954-59.

19 Royal Horse Guards trooper in winter dress; set 1343. Introduced four years after the Life Guards in cloaks, and discontinued in 1959 — thus making them slightly more scarce — this example can be dated to the late 1930s. Note that the reins were not painted post-war.

20 Horse Guards Standard Bearer at the Halt. Using the same casting as the trooper, this was only available in Picture Pack 1339B.

39

Dragoon Guards and Dragoons by Britains, UK

1

2

3

6

7

8

12

13

14

In the late 17th century dragoons were mounted infantry armed with heavy muskets known as "dragons", while the true heavy cavalry were known as regiments of horse. From the mid-18th century the regiments of horse were all made into dragoons, purely as an economy measure as dragoons received less pay and rode inferior horses. To lessen the heavy cavalry's resentment they were given the title dragoon guards. The dragoons later became light cavalry. The heavy cavalry wore a Household Cavalry type helmet, in brass for dragoon guards and white metal for dragoons.

1-2 1st King's Dragoon Guards; set 2074. Trooper on cantering horse,

and officer on trotting grey. The 1st King's Dragoon Guards were not issued as a set of five until 1953. They had been depicted in a large Display Set no. 129 from 1902-30, mounted on trotting horses, but this version is rare. Note that for this late-version officer (2) Britains went to the trouble of snipping off part of the carbine casting, which of course an officer would not have carried. All ranks, including the officer, have the late-pattern sword arm with gauntlet, also used by the Household Cavalry. It is possible to find the trooper on a trotting head-up brown horse, and the officer on a cantering head-down grey; these were issued in Picture Packs 1279B and 1278B respectively. The 1st King's

Dragoon Guards were well represented in Picture Packs; pack 1341B was a trumpeter on a brown "Scots Grey" horse, with a white plume, and 1342B was a standard bearer on a cantering brown horse.

3 1st King's Dragoon Guards Trooper, Dismounted; Picture Pack 1343B. This unusual figure employs an infantry/Guards officer type body at attention with a Household Cavalry head. It was only available as a Picture Pack from 1954-59.

4-5 The Queen's Bays (2nd Dragoon Guards); set 44. This set was produced from 1896-1952 with the usual break for World War II, and normally contained a trumpeter rather than an officer, as did some other cavalry sets —

although an officer does sometimes turn up. The trooper (4) dates from the 1920s, while the trumpeter rides a galloping grey, date-stamped 1.1.1901. Later trumpeters, more in keeping with the regiment's name, ride trotting bay horses.

6-7 5th Royal Inniskilling Dragoon Guards; set 3. First issued in 1893, this was the next set to be produced by Britains after the Household Cavalry, earlier versions being based on the same figures. In fact the officer always used the same casting as the Household Cavalry officer until this set ceased production in 1940, as shown at (7), but the trooper (6) sits a trotting brown horse. These are late examples. For another version of the 5th Dragoon

40

4

5

9

10

11

15

16

17

Guards see (10-11) *page 90.*

8-9 6th Dragoon Guards; set 106, produced from 1900-40. The troopers of this set, riding galloping black and brown horses, carry carbines and are the only dragoon guards to wear blue jackets. The officer (9) is unique in using the Royal Horse Artillery officer's casting, with a different head, resulting in a fixed-arm figure with superfluous frogging cast on his jacket. The trooper is dated 1.1.1901. These figures should not be confused with the Canadian Governor General's Horse Guards, shown at (28-29) *page 77,* which also have blue uniforms and white plumes.

10-11 7th Dragoon Guards, later 4th/7th Dragoon Guards; set 127, produced from 1902-40. The

troopers are distinguished by their black and white plumes and by their slung lances (which often tend to be lost or broken!) The officer rides a black horse at full gallop. Note that Britains correctly depicted all ranks on black horses; the nickname of the regiment was "The Black Horse".

12-14 1st Dragoons; set 31, in production 1895-1940. The 1st Dragoons officer of 1902-9 (12) uses the Household Cavalry officer's horse as mentioned on *page 38,* here with the black throat plume. The trooper (13) sits a walking horse dated 1.1.1902, of the same type as that ridden by the Scots Greys who were introduced at the same time, and has a helmet with a black vertically-hanging plume. The

later officer (14) on his prancing Household Cavalry-type horse is virtually the same as the officer of the 5th Dragoon Guards except for his black plume, although note that on this example Britains appear to have painted his helmet gold, rather than silver.

15-16 Royal Scots Greys (2nd Dragoons); set 32. In production from 1902-66 these figures of Scotland's only regular cavalry regiment were always popular and thus some of the commonest Britains cavalry to be found. Note that the only difference between the trooper (15) and the officer (16) on these early post-war examples is the officer's extended sword arm and gold collar, cross belt and trouser stripes. In a late four-piece set of

c1960 included an officer on a cantering horse with the sword held vertically, and two troopers mounted on trotting horses. Late Scots Greys' horses have the dappling sprayed rather than brushed on. A rare "half-set" no. 2119 contained a trooper on a cantering horse and two dismounted Scots Greys troopers at attention — similar to the King's Dragoon Guards trooper (3) but in bearskin caps.

17 Scots Greys trooper, with movable plug-in sword arm. A rare early large-scale figure from an unnumbered set of officer, trumpeter and four troopers issued in 1893-4. Mounted on a brown horse, this figure served as the officer to the plug-handed fusilier shown at (1) *page 50.*

Hussars by Britains, UK

1   2   3

7   8   9

14   15   16

In 1811, during the Napoleonic Wars, several light dragoon regiments were converted to hussars, in imitation of Hungarian light cavalry, from which the name was derived. They were distinguished by cylindrical fur busbies with coloured cloth ''bags'' hanging at the sides, much frogging and other exotic touches. Britains made a number of attractive representations of the hussar regiments, using their standard range of cavalry horse positions, so that apart from the dismounted figure, their hussars did not have frogging detail moulded on the tunics; this was indicated by paintwork alone.

1-2 Trooper and officer of the 3rd Hussars; set 13. When first

issued in 1893 the 3rd Hussars used a fixed-arm figure on a small trotting horse, the same as (18), but changed to the cantering horse and the short carbine like (19) in 1903. The trooper illustrated here was produced from 1920-40 with the longer carbine. Post-war, the only way to obtain 3rd Hussars was in the short-lived set 2120, from 1957-59. This comprised one mounted hussar at the halt with sword at the carry, like (13), one dismounted hussar (10), and a horse at the halt. As with most cavalry sets the troopers ride both black and brown horses. The officer (2) uses the Household Cavalry officer's rearing horse. Note that both he and the 11th Hussars officer on the same

mount (8) are correctly depicted with leopard-skin saddle covers.
3-4 Trooper and trumpeter of the 4th Hussars; set 8. This set, with troopers at the gallop, always had a trumpeter rather than an officer and is probably the commonest of the hussar sets to be found, being produced from 1896-1952 as a five-piece set. 4th Hussars were also available right through to 1966 teamed up with the Life Guards in set 50, and pre-war with Royal Horse Guards and standing firing Grenadier Guards in set 53.
5-6 Trooper and officer of the 7th Hussars, set 2075. Introduced as late as 1953, the officer for this set rides the heavy ADC's horse — see (22) *page 91* — while the troopers ride two cantering bay

(mid-brown) horses and two dark brown trotting horses. They all have the late-pattern sword-arm at the carry.
7-8 Trooper and officer of the 11th Hussars; set 12. This regiment, with its unique crimson trousers which earned it the nickname of 'The Cherry-Pickers', was well represented by Britains. Like set 13, depicting the 3rd Hussars, this set was introduced in 1893 using a fixed-arm trooper on the small trotting horse — changed to the cantering horse in 1903 — initially with a short carbine. The officer is mounted on the Household Cavalry rearing horse. This set was available until 1940.
9-10 11th Hussars, Dismounted with Horses; set 182. This very attractive and unusual set,

4

5

6

10

11

12

13

17

18

19

introduced in 1913, contained four saddled horses in black and brown and four dismounted hussars: three empty-handed troopers, and an officer using the same casting but holding a drawn sword.

11-12 11th Hussars, Mounted and Dismounted at the Halt; set 270. This interesting and scarce set available from 1928-40 combined the dismounted hussars and horses from set 182 (9-10) with these new figures of hussars mounted at the halt. Readily identified by their red trousers and busby bags, they are unusual in that both the officer (12) and troopers (11) are portrayed empty-handed — but as if to compensate, they have frogging detail painted on the cuff. The

only difference between the figures is that the officer's busby is slightly smaller with a taller plume, and he has gold frogging, collar and trouser stripes.

13 11th Hussar Trooper at the Halt; Picture Pack 883B. Compared with the trooper in set 270 this 11th Hussar has darker crimson trousers and holds a sword at the carry. The 11th Hussars officer, Picture Pack 647B, was similar to (8) but with the sword at the carry.

14-15 10th Hussars, trooper and officer; set 315. This is the rarest regular set of Britains hussars, as it was only produced for about 12 years between the wars. The figures have red busby bags and white over black plumes, and both the trooper and officer are modelled at the halt with swords

at the carry, using the same casting as the 11th Hussars mounted at the halt in set 270. The only difference between the castings is that the officer's busby is smaller with a taller plume. Note that Britains mounted hussars always seem to have their cap lines (cords to prevent loss of the busby) permanently blowing in a high wind, even when at the halt!

16-17 13th Hussars; set 99, produced from 1899-1940. All ranks ride cantering horses, the officer being distinguished by riding a grey horse and having an extended sword arm. The busby bags on these 1930s examples are white, but Britains sometimes painted them in buff.

18 Middlesex Yeomanry; set 83. This

was not a regular cavalry regiment, but Britains probably produced the figures because of their local connections and attractive uniform. London-based part-time volunteers, their full title was The 1st County of London Yeomanry (Middlesex, the Duke of Cambridge's Hussars). This is the first 1898-1903 fixed-arm version in the distinctive hussar-style uniform, with green tunic and double red trouser stripes. Note that the tip of the carbine is missing on this example.

19 The later Middlesex Yeomanry trooper on a cantering horse, introduced in 1903, with the short-carbine movable arm in use until 1920. From then until 1940 the same trooper was used with a longer carbine.

Lancers by Britains, UK

Lancers were introduced into the British Army just after the Napoleonic Wars, the British having observed the effectiveness of the lance in the hands of Napoleon's Polish Lancers. The light dragoons converted to lancers adopted the Polish square-topped cap as their distinctive headgear and later wore a panel of cloth in facing colour on the front of the tunic, known as a plastron.

1 12th Lancers trooper. This is the very earliest type of Britains lancer, smaller than standard size, on a galloping horse with a plug-in arm that goes right through the torso. This rare figure with red plume and plastron represents a trooper from a set of nine without a number which included an officer and trumpeter.

2 5th Royal Irish Lancers trooper; set 23. Identified by the green plume, this trooper at the halt on the first-version horse was produced from 1894-1903. With the lance and arm as an integral part of the figure, this is an accomplished piece of casting, although the horse's rear legs are rather two-dimensional.

3 Lancer officer. No excuses are needed for showing three examples of the Britains lancer officer turned in the saddle, based on a painting by the eminent Victorian military artist Richard Simkin. This excellent casting was available with only minor alterations right through from 1894-1966, retaining the tin-strip sword throughout. This particular item is an oddity, purporting to be a post-war green-plumed 5th Lancer officer, but Britains did not produce this regiment after the war. Close examination reveals that this is probably a 12th Lancers officer from Picture Pack 1349B with the distinguishing red plume carefully overpainted in green. It is typical of the problems encountered when identifying Britains figures.

4 5th Lancers Trooper; set 23. This is a second-version lancer with movable lance arm, on the improved horse at the halt. Introduced in 1903, this set was dropped in the early 1930s, the 5th Lancers having amalgamated with the 16th Lancers.

5 9th Queen's Royal Lancers officer; set 24. A post-war officer turned in the saddle, identifiable by the black and white plume. Still with the tin-strip sword, this example dates from the 1960s.

6 9th Lancers trooper at the halt; set 24 (post-war). This set had previously used the same castings as (2) from 1894-1903, and then those of (4) from 1903-40, with the lance at the carry. When reintroduced after World War II the 9th troopers carried slung lances as shown.

7 12th Lancers trooper; set 128. This set, produced from 1902-40, had troopers on cantering horses and an officer on a trotting grey.

8 12th Lancers; set 2076. This new set of 12th Lancers was introduced in 1953. Like other sets of that period, the troopers

were on two patterns of horse — cantering and trotting — and held their lances at the carry. In contrast to the pre-war version the officer rides a cantering grey with his sword vertical.

9 12th Lancers officer; set 128. Unlike the officer from set 2076 at (8) this officer from the late 1930s has an outstretched sword arm and rides a grey at the trot.

10 16th Lancers trooper; set 33. While all other British lancer regiments wore basically dark blue uniforms the 16th were resplendent in red tunics with blue plastrons. This is the first version at the halt, produced from 1895-1903, with a fixed arm, and is the same basic casting as (2).

11 16th/5th Lancers trooper; set 33. In contrast with (10), a late

version trooper from this very attractive set's brief post-war revival from 1946-52.

12 16th/5th Lancers officer; set 33. The magnificent officer turned in the saddle, this time in the red tunic of the 16th Lancers in a post-war issue. Note that the 16th Lancers had amalgamated with the 5th Lancers in 1922 and Britains dropped the latter from the range a few years later. The 16th took precedence in the amalgamated title because of some indiscretion committed by the 5th Lancers in the past.

13 21st Empress of India's Lancers in Full Dress; set 100. A trooper in the attractive blue/grey plastron and white plume of this famous regiment, dating from the 1930s.

14 21st Lancers trumpeter; set 100.

This set contained a trumpeter on a grey cantering horse, rather than an officer.

15 21st Lancers trooper, armed with a sword! This oddity turns up from time to time and is original — he does not have a replacement arm, and does not appear to be intended as an officer as he has neither gold trim nor an extended sword arm. He was probably intended for sale singly as a second-grade figure. Two distinct versions of the 21st Lancers in service dress were also available under set number 94: as "Heroes of Omdurman and Khartoum" in khaki with foreign service helmets, from 1898, as at (19) *page 55*, and later in World War I steel helmets as at (18, 19) *pages 84-85*.

16 17th Lancers trooper in active service dress; set 81. Known as Ulundi Lancers as they depict the 17th Lancers at that battle in the Zulu War, this set was first introduced in 1897. They are in white foreign service helmets, but otherwise in full dress with their distinctive white plastrons.

17 17th Lancers trumpeter; set 81. This set normally included a trumpeter on a trotting bay rather than an officer. When an officer was included the excellent casting of an officer turned in the saddle was used, complete with a full dress lancer cap. These two figures date from shortly before the set's deletion in 1940. 17th Lancers were also available in full dress with lancer caps in the Display Set 73.

The excellent gun teams produced by Britains in different versions have always been very popular with collectors.

1 Royal Horse Artillery Gun Team at the Gallop; set 39. This is the version produced from 1895-1906, the distinctive features being the shafted limber and the gunners riding on the gun and limber. Whereas all later limbers have a centre pole only, in this pattern the offside wheeler (the unridden horse nearest to the limber) is harnessed between a central shaft and a side shaft running forward from the right-hand wheel hub. The hinged limber top has valises at the ends, and slots to hold two seated gunners. Plug-in seats on the axle tree of the gun also hold seated gunners. The gun resembles a 15-pounder of the period.

2-5 Royal Horse Artillery Gun Team; set 39, second version (1906-25). This revised version reflected changes in real artillery practice. The limber was altered to a centrepole type, shown at (7), and to lighten the load the seated gunners were replaced by mounted outriders. A mounted officer was also added. The outriders on trotting horses (2-4) carry short carbines and look like hussars, but they have short jackets — note the red trouser stripe continued up to the waist — and their horses have painted-on breast harness. The RHA mounted officer (5) is a fixed-arm figure with frogging detail cast on his jacket, on a galloping horse.

6 Royal Field Artillery; set 144. This represents heavier artillery than the RHA, and a walking team is used. The mounted gunners have two patterns of movable whip arm. The men seated on the gun were soon dropped, but the men on the limber were retained, no mounted outriders being provided with this set. A mounted officer (not shown) rode a brown cantering horse.

7-12 Royal Horse Artillery Khaki Gun Team; set 39a (later 1339). Introduced in 1919, this set depicts the RHA in the service uniform of World War I. The only change to the castings is the replacement of busbies by peaked caps, although the magnificence of full dress has

Right: *Mountain Gun of the Royal Artillery; set 28. This is a late example, from 1965, of a very popular and attractive set that was introduced in 1895. The set comprised a mounted officer and six gunners in white foreign service helmets, dark blue tunics and pale khaki breeches, with four mules carrying the three parts of the mountain gun and a load of ammunition.*

been replaced by khaki. Apart from the peaked cap, the officer (8) is the same casting as the full-dress version, resulting in incorrect frogging cast on his khaki tunic. The outriders (9-12) follow the same formula; note that they have the longer carbines newly introduced by Britains.

13-18 King's Troop Royal Artillery; set 39. This early post-war example uses a finely-detailed limber with a hinged rear section, and a gun loosely based on a late 18-pounder, both introduced in 1930. The horses wear the light breast harness which replaced the heavy collar harness on Britains gun teams in 1925, and are linked by plain wire. In about 1950 this was replaced by light brown painted H-shaped clips which could be readily removed and replaced. The trotting outriders have been replaced by figures at the full gallop (14-17), similar to the 4th Hussars. This set still has the original pattern officer (18) but about this time a new officer with a plain movable arm was introduced.

19-24 Royal Horse Artillery, Active Service; (B series) set 126. From about 1898 Britains produced a range of soldiers smaller than their "standard" infantryman size of 54mm (2.12in), known as the B series. In this range (dealt with more fully on *pages 92-93*), infantrymen were 44mm (1.73in) high. This set, and the full dress gun team, set 125, appeared in 1901. The field gun has a strip of spring steel which can be flexed to fire projectiles. The officer (20) rides a grey at the gallop, and has a movable outstretched sword arm. The outriders (21-24) use the same casting, but with a carbine arm and black or brown horses. The full dress outrider is shown at (32) on *page 93*. Both sets stayed in the catalogue until 1939.

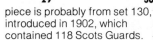

Britains Foot Guards have always been popular sellers, with the result that they are some of the commonest figures to be found today. The identifying plume colours of the Guards are: Grenadier Guards: white plume on the left. Coldstream Guards: red plume on the right. Scots Guards: no plume. Irish Guards: blue plume on the right — but note Britains at first used green. Welsh Guards: white plume with green bar across, on the left.

1 Grenadier Guards, Standing Firing; set 34. This is the first version, fixed-arm officer with gaiters, on an oval base, who was accompanied by eight guardsmen firing and a drummer boy in the original 1895-1901 set. See (4).

2 Colours and Pioneers of the Scots Guards; set 82. A first-version (1897-1905) pioneer from a set of seven with a colour bearer.

3 Irish Guards; set 107. This first-version Irish Guardsman, marching at the slope with (incorrect) green plume, was introduced soon after the regiment's actual formation in 1900. Note this is the same as (2) but with a "droopy sling" rifle.

4 Grenadier Guards, Standing Firing; set 34. This is the first-version firing Guardsman of 1895-1901, "volley firing".

5 Scots Guards; set 75. This is the third-version square-based marching Scots Guardsman of about 1908, date-stamped 1.8.1905, which refers to the same figure on an oval base.

6 Scots Guards, Running at the Trail; set 70. Introduced in 1899, this was a short-lived set, using the first-version running figure.

7 Irish Guardsman running at the trail, from display set 102. This is the final-version running at the trail figure, with the left arm close to the body.

8 Coldstream Guards officer on "sway-back" horse. This figure usually appeared in set 111, as a Grenadier Guards officer with men at attention. As a Coldstream it is probably from Display Set 93.

9 Irish Guards officer; from set 102, see also (7). A rather battered figure, dated 1.1.1901, based on the cavalry horse at the gallop.

10 Scots Guards officer, mounted on a brown version of the Scots Greys' horse. This interesting

piece is probably from set 130, introduced in 1902, which contained 118 Scots Guards.

11-12 Grenadier Guards in Winter Overcoats; set 312. An officer and man from 1929-66.

13-15 Grenadier Guards Firing; set 34. The different items from a nine-piece version of this set, from the late 1930s. Compare with (1) and (4).

16 Kneeling Guards officer. Up to 1940 this officer could be found with a red plume in set 120: Coldstream Guards Kneeling Firing, or with a blue plume in set 124: Irish Guards Lying Firing. As a Scots Guards officer this may be from set 130 — see (10).

17-18 Coldstream Guards at Present; set 205. The two versions of Guardsmen presenting arms

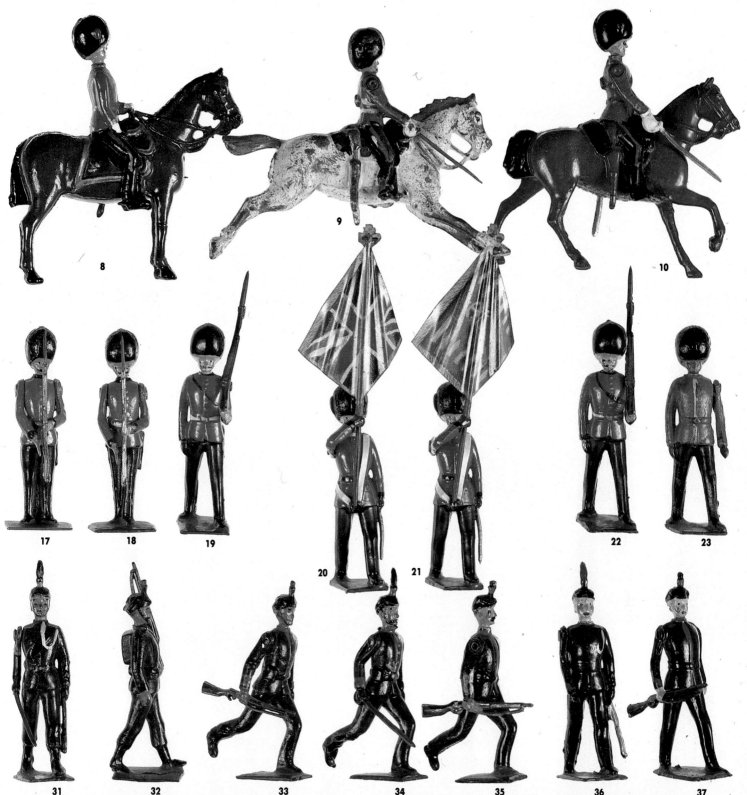

8

9

10

17   18   19   20   21   22   23

31   32   33   34   35   36   37

produced from 1923-40; (17) has the feet together while the later version (18) has the right foot brought back at an angle.

19-22 Grenadier Guards Colour Party; set 460. The two ensigns and two of the colour sergeants from a set of seven pieces produced as Grenadier Guards from 1932-35, and then with the same set number as Scots Guards until 1940.

23 An unusual Scots Guards officer based on a Guardsman casting. This rather battered example has a plain left arm, maroon waist sash, gold collar and cuffs, and brown gloves, and is presumably from set 130.

24-25 Scots Guards; set 75. A 1930s Guardsman and officer from a set that lasted from 1897-1965. A

piper (27) was also included.

26 Scots Guards pioneer with axe; set 82, final version, from the 1946-59 period. Compare with (2).

27 Scots Guards piper; set 76. To avoid confusion with Black Watch pipers, note that while both have feather bonnets with red hackles and Royal Stuart tartan, the Scots Guards pipers have dark blue doublets and the Black Watch dark green.

28 One of six pipers from set 2096: Drum and Pipe Band of the Irish Guards. This unusual figure wears a dark green tunic and caubeen from which a small blue plume is missing on this example, and a plain brown kilt. This set was produced from 1954-65.

29 Scots Guardsman at attention. Up to 1940 this figure was

produced as a grenadier in set 111, while from 1954 the pose was used to represent Coldstream Guards in set 2082. A Scots Guardsman was available post-war in a Picture Pack, but that shown here is in the pre-war paint style so must be from the large Display Set 130.

30 Coldstream Guardsman at ease; set 314, produced from 1929-40. Post-war this casting was used for the Welsh Guards in set 2083.

31-32 The Rifle Brigade; set 9, produced from 1897-1915. From their formation in the Napoleonic Wars to carry rifled weapons rather than smooth-bore muskets, the rifle regiments have been associated with dark green uniforms. Britains produced the Rifle Brigade with black facings,

and the Rifle Corps with red facings. This officer and man have square bases dated 16.11.1905 and 1.8.1905 respectively.

33-35 The Kings Royal Rifle Corps; set 98, introduced in 1899. (33) and (34) are the square-based first-version rifleman and officer with a gap between the left arm and the body. (35) is the later, rather inferior casting with the left arm tight against the body.

36-37 Kings Royal Rifle Corps Marching at the Trail; set 2072. After a brief post-war revival, set 98 was replaced in 1953 by this set of riflemen marching at the trail. The officer (36) uses the standard 1930 body while the rifleman (37) is based on the US Marine casting.

1 2 3 4 5 6

14 15 16 17 18 19 20

28 29 30 31 32

The full dress uniform of the British line infantry, as worn from 1879-1914, and depicted by Britains, consisted of scarlet tunic, dark blue trousers and spiked helmet. The fusiliers — whose name derives from an early improved musket, the fusil, which was only issued to special units — had as their distinctive headgear a cap similar to the Guards' bearskin, but smaller and and made of seal or racoon skin.

1 The "Plug-handed Fusilier". Possibly the first foot figure to be produced by Britains, this rare 60mm (2.36in) fusilier steps off on the right foot on a plain square base, and has a separate rifle that plugs into the left cuff. The only figure with which it is compatible

is the large Scots Grey — see (17) *page 41* — which, on a brown horse, was used as an officer in an unnumbered set with fusiliers.
2 Royal Sussex Regiment; set 36. This figure is rather undersized at 50mm (2in), oval-based, but without gaiters, and commits the military sin of sloping arms on the right shoulder.
3 Infantry officer. This is the first-version fixed-arm officer with medal detail and the very small head sometimes used at this time. Probably from the Buffs (11-13), but Britains did not put facing colours on their officers, making identification difficult.
4-5 7th Royal Fusiliers; set 7. Two views of the 1897-1905 round-based movable-arm figure.
6 The Royal West Surrey Regiment.

The 1905 infantry figure with Slade-Wallace equipment and oval base, replaced by a square base three years later. The Surreys were normally portrayed "at the ready" with fixed bayonets, but were also marching at the slope in Display Set 29.
7-10 Somersetshire Light Infantry; set 17. The elements of a ten-piece set that contained an officer, bugler, four standing and four kneeling figures, introduced in 1894, but with the short-lived movable-arm "wasp waisted" officer introduced about four years later. The SLI have green Light Infantry helmets.
11-13 The Buffs (East Kent Regiment); set 16. Another ten-piece set, containing an officer, bugler, drummer boy and seven

men at the ready, with buff facings. The officer (11) is the improved 1905 figure matching the infantryman at (6).
14-15 The Warwickshire Regiment at the Present; set 206. An officer and man presenting arms, from an eight-piece set. The first, 1923 version had the legs at attention, but this second version has the right leg brought back.
16-17 East Yorkshire Regiment; set 113. (16) is the first version, introduced in 1901, of a set of eight round-based gaitered infantrymen at attention, each with a right-angled arm holding the rifle near the muzzle. A later square-based version (17) was introduced c1908, with the final-type straight arm holding the rifle into the side of the body.

| 7 | 8 | 9 | 10 | 11 | 12 | 13 |

| 21 | 22 | 23 | 24 | 25 | 26 | 27 |

| 33 | 34 | 35 | 36 | 37 | 38 | 39 |

18-20 Royal Irish Regiment, Standing, Kneeling and Lying Firing; set 156. A set of ten, later eight line infantry with blue facings. These gaitered figures are the first version of 1908.

21 The Buffs; set 16. The second-version square-based "on guard" figure with gaiters of 1910-30.

22 The Worcestershire Regiment; set 18. Using the same castings as set 17 (7-10) this set was usually distinguished by white helmets and facings. This unusual late example, "kneeling to receive cavalry", has a blue helmet and dark green facings.

23-24 Queens Royal Regiment (West Surrey); set 2086. Post-war, the full-trousered infantrymen in firing positions introduced about 1930 were available in this 16-piece

set, with an officer holding binoculars. Note that the full-trousered lying figure (24) has the legs splayed, unlike the earlier gaitered figure.

25-27 The York and Lancaster Regiment Running at the Trail; set 96. (25) is the "pigeon-chested" first version introduced in 1899, but note that this example is later as it does not have the earlier magazine rifle. The second version (26) has full trousers and "daylight" between the left arm and the body. The officer (27) is the same figure as the man but with an outstretched sword arm and gold facings.

28-29 The Middlesex Regiment; set 76. This post-war officer and man, produced until 1963, are from a set introduced in 1897. They use

the final form of marching figure.

30 Royal Sussex Regiment; set 36. An early example of the 1910 marching infantryman figure, with a "droopy sling" rifle, blue facings and the white helmet in which Britains were to portray the Royal Sussex until 1940.

31-32 Royal Sussex Regiment; set 36. An infantryman and mounted officer from the post-war set of six men and an officer, now with blue helmets. The officer uses the heavy ADC's horse.

33 Fusilier; a gaitered square-based version from the late 1920s. Britains made no distinction between their 7th Royal Fusiliers, set 7, and Royal Welch Fusiliers, set 74, except for the inclusion of a goat mascot with the latter. The Royal Welch Fusiliers lasted

right through to the end, but the Royal Fusiliers set was discontinued in 1940.

34-36 Royal Welch Fusiliers; set 74. (34-35) are two views of the final pattern fusilier produced in about 1930. Note that the fusiliers kept their full equipment when they lost their gaiters. (36) is the final-pattern officer, full-trousered and empty-handed, from the 1930s.

37 The splendid long-haired goat mascot of the Royal Welch Fusiliers, with gilded horns and a shield on his forehead.

38-39 The Royal Welch Fusiliers at Attention; from set 2124. This rare set contained an officer, two men and the goat mascot, and was only produced from 1957-59. Note that the fusilier (39) is used as the scale man in this book.

Scottish Troops by Britains, UK

1   2   3   4   5   6   7

16   17   18   19   20

27   28   29   30   31

1-2 The Black Watch; set 11. These rather stocky figures running at the trail on plain oval bases are from Britains' first set of Highlanders. Note that the same casting is used for officer and man; they have weapons with hands that plug into the cuff of the figure. The Black Watch are distinguished by red frackles in their bonnets and dark green kilts with black hatching. This version was produced from 1893-1903.

3 The Argyll and Sutherland Highlanders; set 15. As set 11, but with yellow facings and a dark green kilt with light green stripes.

4 The Seaforth Highlanders; set 112. This marching Highlander in full equipment with movable arm is from a set without an officer introduced in 1901. Seaforths

have red and white stripes over dark green kilts.

5 Gordon Highlanders; set 77. A private from a set introduced in 1897 which included two pipers. Gordons have yellow cross-hatching over dark green kilts.

6 Cameron Highlanders (Active Service); set 114. Introduced in 1901 during the Boer War, this set uses the same body casting as (4-5) but with a foreign service helmet and khaki jacket. This example has the early smooth helmet, which was soon replaced. The Camerons have dark blue kilts with red and yellow stripes.

7 Black Watch Highlanders; set 122. An early undated oval-based figure from a set available from 1901-40, consisting initially of nine men standing firing and a

standing officer with binoculars.

8-12 The Cameron Highlanders; set 89. This 30-piece set containing the new Highlander figures in firing positions was introduced in 1901. Available until 1940, it consisted of a standing officer with binoculars (8), a kneeling officer (10), six men standing firing (9), nine men kneeling firing (11), ten men lying firing (12), and two pipers in glengarries.

13-15 The Gordon Highlanders; these were available as lying firing figures from 1901 in set 118 (15), and in all three firing positions from 1908 in set 157.

16 Argyll and Sutherland Highlanders; set 15. In 1903 the "plug handed" Highlander was replaced by a vigorously charging figure. The oval base changed to

a square base in 1908, this example dating from the 1930s.

17 The Black Watch; set 11. The same casting as (16), from a post-war set reduced to five charging Highlanders, but with the addition of the marching piper (34).

18-20 Seaforth Highlanders Charging with Mounted Officer and Pipers; set 2062. The pre-war large set of Seaforths, no. 88, was not reinstated after the war, but replaced in 1952 by this set of 14 charging Highlanders (18), two pipers in dark green doublets and glengarries (19) and the excellent mounted officer (20).

21-22 Officers of the Gordon Highlanders; set 437. When first produced, these excellent figures of Highland officers mounted in trews, and marching in kilt and

52

plaid, were only available as Gordons, and were not introduced into the existing sets of Highlanders. They were available from 1932-40.

23 Officer of the Argyll and Sutherland Highlanders. This is a Britains special painting, just the same as the Gordon officer (22), but with light green cross-hatching on kilt and plaid.

24 Gordon Highlander Officer; Picture Pack 461B. A direct comparison can be made between this post-war version, only available in a Picture Pack, and the same figure from the pre-war set 437 (22).

25 Seaforth Highlander officer. This post-war figure is something of a puzzle as Britains did not normally produce a marching

Seaforth officer; he is from set 1323 which normally contained Royal Fusiliers and Royal Sussex Regiment with officers, and Seaforth Highlanders without — but occasionally, as here, a Seaforth officer was included.

26 Seaforth Highlanders; set 112. This is the bulkier figure without equipment which replaced the earlier marching Highlander (4) just before World War I.

27 Highlander; 34N. This is the standing firing Highlander in a second-grade khaki paint finish.

28-29 Highlanders in khaki, running. These Highlanders in glengarries, charging in two positions and slightly over-scale, are pre-war second-grade items.

30-31 Highlanders, Khaki, Charging with Bayonets; Shrapnel-proof

Helmets. These are the same as (28-29) but with steel helmets.

32 Cameron Highlanders (Active Service); set 114. Like the marching full dress Highlanders this set also changed to the bigger figure without equipment in about 1914, but with a foreign service helmet and khaki tunic. Available until 1940, and 1946-47.

33 Black Watch Highlander; set 449. A rare paint version of the marching Highlander, issued briefly in the 1930s.

34 Black Watch piper: this post-war piper was available in set 11 with five charging Black Watch from 1946, in Display Set 73, and set 2109: Highland Pipe Band of the Black Watch, shown on *page 83*.

35 Black Watch marching officer; an extra-fine quality "special"

painting of the Highland officer.

36 Highland Light Infantry; set 213. In 1924 Britains produced a figure in Scottish doublet and trews to represent the non-kilted Scottish regiments. The HLI have their distinctive shakoes and green trews with red and white stripes. Not available post-war.

37 The Royal Scots; set 212. Introduced at the same time as the HLI, this set used the same body with a Kilmarnock bonnet. Early examples have yellow criss-cross stripes over dark green on the trews. This later version has red and white stripes over green.

38 Royal Scots piper. When set 212 was revived in 1948, reduced to five pieces, it included this piper in green doublet, Royal Stuart tartan and a glengarry.

Boer War Troops by Britains, UK

1 2 3 4 5 6

12 13

16 17 18

The outbreak of the Boer War in 1899 led to a number of new releases from Britains, now all highly prized and a field of collecting in their own right.

1-4 The Buffs; set 16. At first, until specially designed figures were available, the scarlet-coated set of Buffs was turned out in khaki uniforms and light brown equipment, under the same set number. See (11-13) *page 51*.

5-6 City Imperial Volunteers; set 104. Although the stance of the infantryman (5) is similar to that of the Buffs at the ready (4), these were entirely new and quite accurate representations of the famous unit of London volunteers. The officer shown is square-based, but the oval-based men

were the first to carry paper copyright labels dated 1900. At first containing ten pieces, later nine, this set lasted until 1940.

7-11 Boer Infantry; set 26. Although the Boers practically all fought in civilian dress, Britains depicted them in light khaki uniforms with black hats, using the same castings as the US Army figures shown at (1-4) *page 78*. The first Boer infantry (7-8) are a different painting of the US infantry figures introduced in 1898 for the Spanish-American War. In 1906 the contents of this set were replaced by an officer using the City Imperial Volunteers casting (11) and two new figures, also used for US infantry, dated 15.6.1906. These were fixed-arm figures at "shoulder arms" (9)

and "at the ready" (10); they were out of the catalogue by about 1910, and are consequently rare.

12-13 Doctor Jameson and the South African Mounted Infantry; set 38. The name of the Administrator of Rhodesia who led an ill-conceived raid into the Transvaal in 1897 was soon dropped from the label, but this set — which changed to a movable-arm version in 1927 — lasted until 1940. See (6) *page 56*.

14-15 Boer Cavalry; set 6. This set used the same castings as set 38, but with light khaki uniforms, black hats and orange facings.

16 Inniskilling Dragoons, Active Service Order; set 108. This attractive one-piece casting was introduced in 1900 and used only for this set and set 105.

17-18 Imperial Yeomanry; set 105.

London's volunteer cavalry in South Africa were portrayed by the same casting as that used for the Inniskilling Dragoons, but with a slouch hat. The officer (18) rides a grey horse. Both figures, which have been slightly retouched, are dated 1.6.1900. This and set 108 were to last until 1940.

19 21st Lancers, in Khaki; set 94. This set of lancers at the gallop actually pre-dates the Boer War; they were introduced in 1898, and the box label refers to them as "Heroes of Omdurman and Khartoum".

20 Gloucestershire Regiment in Khaki; set 119. Introducing a new standing firing figure in a Wolseley helmet and puttees, this set of ten, later eight, men was produced from 1901-39.

7   **8**   **9**   **10**   **11**

14   **15**

19   **20**   **21**   **22**   **23**   **24**

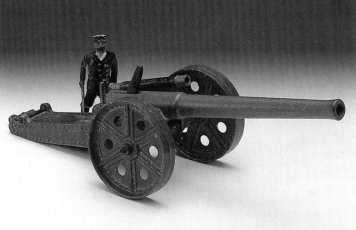

Left: *4.7-inch Naval Gun; set 1264. First produced in the 1900s, this did not gain a set number until 1933. With the army in South Africa desperately short of heavy firepower, the Royal Navy dismounted some 4.7-inch guns from its warships and ran up field mountings for them out of boiler plate. Britains captured very well the look of this long-barrelled weapon with its massively constructed wheels.*

21 York and Lancasters; set 96. Like the Buffs (1-4) this is an example of a scarlet-coated line infantry set, shown at (25) *page 51*, which was produced for a while in khaki, in this case with white equipment and black boots and gaiters. This is a rare figure.

22 CFE Army Service Supply Column. A scarce figure using the same body casting as the Dublin Fusiliers and Devonshires, but with a slouch hat. Ten of these, with an officer mounted on a walking horse, formed the escort for two GS wagons with supplies, made by Britains for sale by the firm of CFE.

23 Dublin Fusiliers; set 109. Introduced in 1901, this is a good representation of a British infantryman in the Boer War marching at the trail. Note the magazine rifle. See (7) *page 84*.

24 Devonshire Regiment; set 110. This is the same as the Dublin Fusiliers, but with a rifle at the slope on the right shoulder, incorrect for the British Army but acceptable on campaign!

Colonial Army Troops by Britains, UK

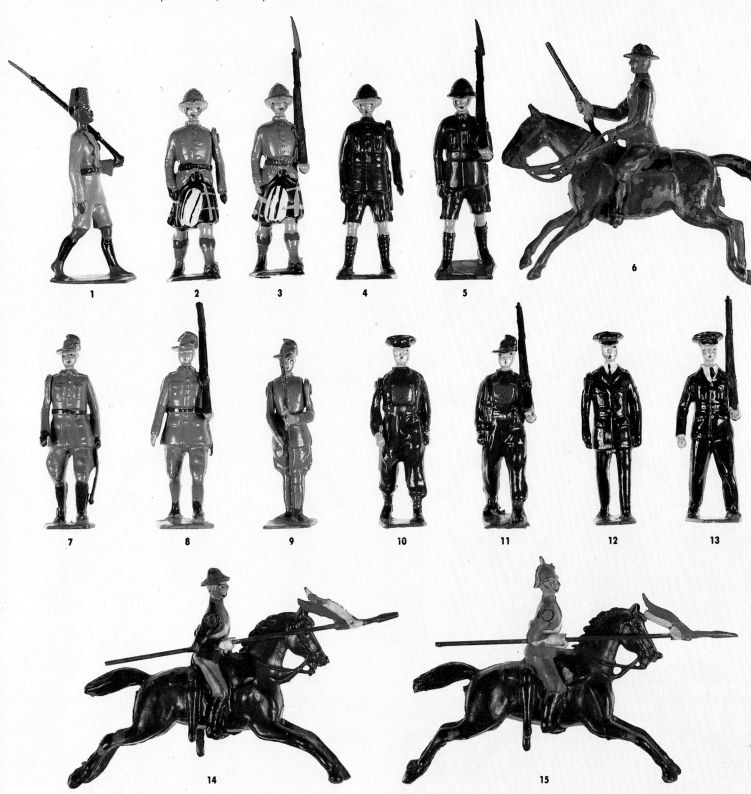

1

2

3

4

5

6

7

8

9

10

11

12

13

14

15

After World War II, those sets shown here that were still in production were listed in the catalogue under "The British Commonwealth of Nations", with the exception of Egypt, listed under "Armies of the World".

1 King's African Rifles; set 225. Introduced in 1925, without an officer, this figure was available in the one version with minor changes in painting style until 1959, and for one last fling in 1966 in the seven-piece set 9162.
2-3 South Africa, Capetown Highlanders; set 1901. Introduced in 1940, this attractive set was the only South African one to have a more than brief post-war appearance, lasting until 1959. The officer (2) has a plain left arm,

brown gloves and waist belt.
4-5 The Regiment Louw Wepener; set 1900. Available only in 1940-41, and 1948-49, effectively for export only, this is a rare and sought-after set, based on set 1294: British Infantry in Tropical Dress, shown at (8-9) *page 84*.
6 South African Mounted Infantry; set 38. A second-version trooper with movable arm holding a rifle; this replaced the fixed-arm type shown at (12-13) *page 54* as late as 1927. This figure uses the same casting as set 1349: Royal Canadian Mounted Police, shown at (18-19) *page 77*, and it is now quite rare.
7-8 Australian Infantry, Service Dress; set 1544. This attractive set used the same body castings as the German Infantry in set 432

shown at (7-10) *page 73*, but with a slouch hat with a grey plume. It was produced from 1937-40 with a brief revival from 1946-48.
9 Australian Infantry, at Present Arms; set 1545. This unusual, rather slight figure shows an Australian at the salute with slouch hat, khaki tunic and breeches. The officer is the same casting with a drawn sword in the right hand and scabbard in the left. Quite hard to find, this set was produced from 1937-40.
10-11 Australian Infantry, in Battledress; set 2031. Introduced in 1949 for an 11-year run, these figures utilize the castings from set 1858: British Infantry, Battledress, shown at (37-38) *page 85*, but provided with slouch hats for the infantrymen (11) and

a peaked cap for the officer (10).
12-13 Australian Infantry, 1948-pattern Blue Ceremonial Dress; set 2030. They wear a dark blue uniform similar to the British No.1 Dress, but with an open collar displaying a white shirt and black tie. The officer (12) uses the casting later used for the US Air Corps officer, set 2044, shown at (20-21) *page 79*. Like set 2031 these figures were available from 1949-59.
14-15 South Australian Lancers; set 49. The Adelaide Lancers, a volunteer unit from South Australia, sent a contingent to take part in Queen Victoria's Diamond Jubilee Procession in 1897, and Britains produced a set of them under the name of South Australian Lancers. Unfortunately

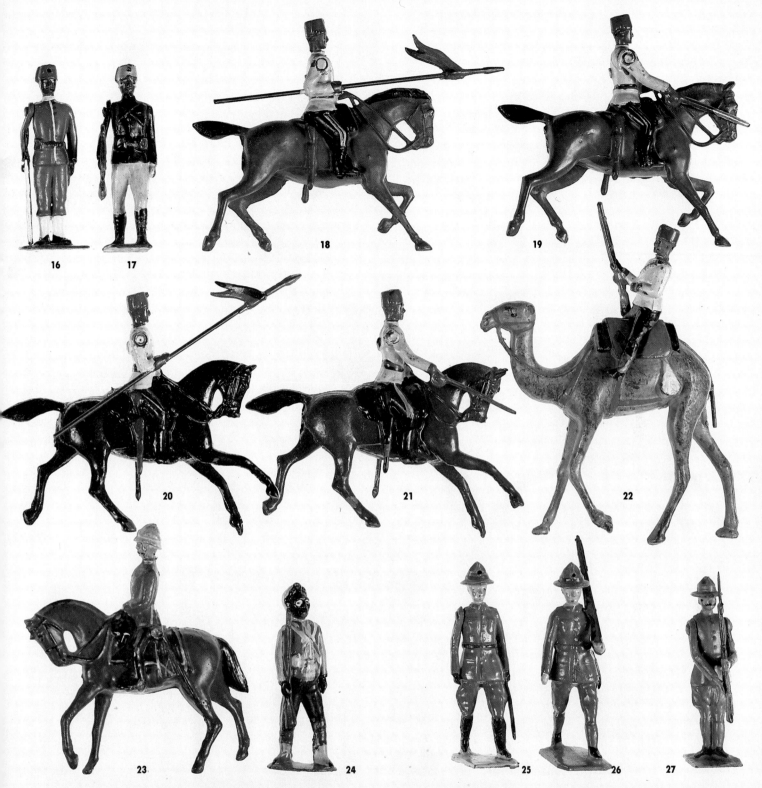

16 17 18 19 20 21 22 23 24 25 26 27

the first version was wrong, having a slouch hat and a full-dress blue lancers tunic with red plastron (14). Britains soon realized their mistake and brought out a corrected version, making the first type very rare. The second version (15) has the correct spiked foreign service helmet and khaki uniform with a red plastron.

16 Egyptian Infantry; set 117. Introduced in 1901, this figure uses the same body casting as the East Yorkshires, shown at (16-17) *page 50*, but in blue-grey with a red fez.

17 Sudanese Infantry; set 116. Produced from 1901-40, without an officer, these troops are based on the Dublin Fusiliers casting shown at (23) *page 55*.

18-21 Egyptian Cavalry; set 115. These figures wear red fezzes, all-white lancer-style tunics, blue breeches, and red and green girdles and lance pennants. The officer is distinguished only by his outstretched sword arm. The first-version Egyptian cavalry (18-19), mounted on what is known as the "pony horse", were only produced from 1901-3, making this version fairly scarce. The second version on the 1903 cantering horse (20-21) had a much longer life, lasting right through to 1966, but reduced to a four-piece set in 1960.

22 Egyptian Camel Corps; set 48. This imposing ensemble consists of a fixed-arm detachable rider with the butt of his rifle resting on his thigh, dressed similarly to the

Egyptian cavalryman but with a brown bandolier and grey leggings. He sits on a rather skinny camel with a wire tail. From 1896-1940 the set consisted of six camels and riders; when reintroduced after the Suez Crisis it had three riders on three camels, and from 1960-66 it was reduced to three camels with only two riders. Later-version camels have a tail cast against the leg instead of a piece of wire.

23-24 The West India Regiment; set 19. A contingent of this regiment were present at Queen Victoria's Diamond Jubilee procession in 1897, but Britains may have produced these figures at an earlier date. The infantryman (24) is a rather short fixed-arm figure

at the shoulder arms, in Zouave-style dress. Early nine-piece sets had a white-helmeted fixed-arm foot officer similar to (3) *page 50*, but this was soon replaced by the fixed-arm mounted officer (23). The set was produced until 1940.

25-26 New Zealand Infantry, Service Dress; set 1542. Introduced in 1937, these figures are (like the Australians) based on the German infantry, but with "boy scout" hats — the first version of which was smaller, as (27). They were available until 1959.

27 New Zealand Infantry, Present Arms; set 1543. This figure is the same as the Australian presenting arms (9) but with the small New Zealand pattern hat; it had the same short run from 1937-40, making it quite scarce.

Indian Army Troops by Britains, UK

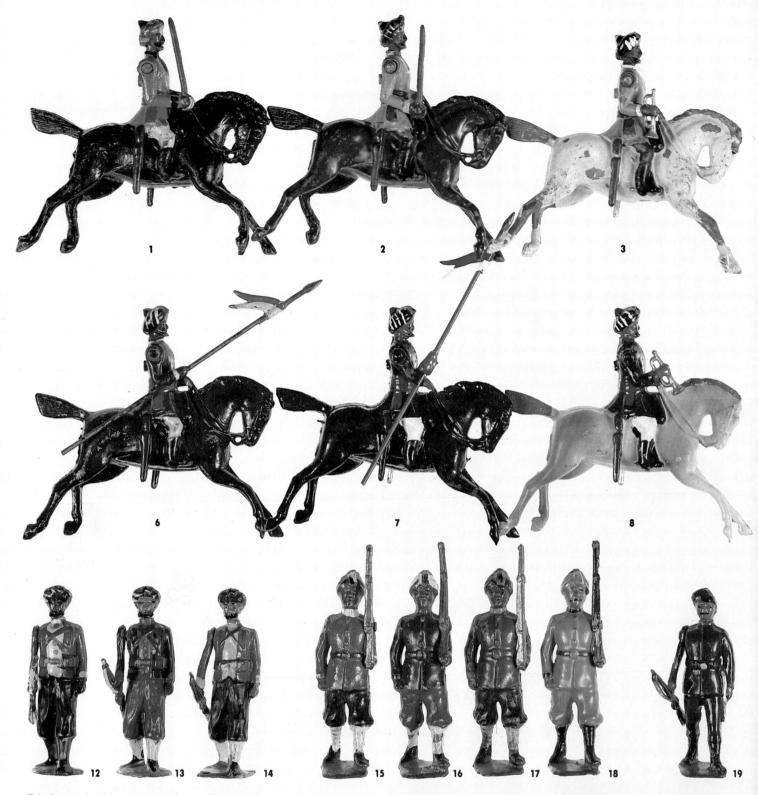

1

2

3

6

7

8

12 13 14 15 16 17 18 19

Britains produced some attractive Indian Army figures, but based on surprisingly few castings. They only used one pattern of horse and rider for all their cavalry, and never modernized it from the original "one-eared" version.

1 1st Bengal Cavalry, later Skinner's Horse; set 47. Like most of Britains' Indian Army figures, this set was first issued in 1896, as a set of four sowars (or troopers) and a trumpeter on a grey horse. Initially they were in mustard-brown "kurtas" (Indian style tunics) with orange-red turbans and cummerbunds, and armed with swords. In the 1930s the set title changed to Skinner's Horse — see (9) and (11).

2-3 3rd Madras Light Cavalry, later

28th Light Cavalry, finally 7th Light Cavalry; set 45. This set contained four sowars with swords (2) and a trumpeter on a grey horse (3). It was available from 1896-1940.

4-5 10th Bengal Lancers, later Hodson's Horse; set 46. In dark blue, with red collar plastrons and cummerbunds, the sowars (4) are armed with lances; unusually, these have red over blue pennants. This set contained a trumpeter, but an officer (5) could be obtained in the ten-piece set 63, from 1896-1940.

6-8 1st Bombay Lancers, later the 13th Duke of Connaught's Own Lancers; set 66. This set of four sowars and a trumpeter had a long life; with uniform changes, they were produced from

1896-1966, losing one figure in 1960. The early version uniform (6) was dark green with white facings, later changing to red facings. Post-war, retitled the 13th Duke of Connaught's Own Lancers, they were given a dark blue uniform with red facings, but no plastron, unlike Hodson's Horse. (7) and (8) are quite late post-war examples.

9,11 Skinner's Horse (1st Duke of York's Own Cavalry); set 47. These are late examples from about 1960 of a sowar (9) and trumpeter (11).

10 Bikanir Camel Corps; set 123. Produced from 1901-40, this set of three men and three camels used the same camel and rider — but with a turbaned head — as the Egyptian Camel Corps

figures shown at (22) *page 57.*

12 1st Madras Native Infantry; set 67. The first-version oval-based infantryman at the trail, from an eight-piece set introduced in 1896. The officer was based on the same figure, with an extended sword arm, and a pioneer was sometimes included as well.

13 2nd Bombay Native Infantry; set 68. Using the same figure as set 67 (12) this set was attired in a dark blue jacket with red facings and front panel, and red baggy trousers. Although an attractive uniform, this is an instance where Britains got it wrong! The 2nd Bombay would actually have looked similar to the 1st Madras, without the white front panel.

14 7th Bengal Infantry; set 64. These are similar to the 1st Madras, but

with a yellow collar, cuffs and front panel to the jacket, and white leggings. They were only available in set 64, which comprised eight of these figures and five 2nd Madras Lancers (not illustrated). The 2nd Madras Lancers (later the 16th Light Cavalry) wore a uniform similar to the 3rd Madras Light Cavalry, but with purple cummerbunds, and carried lances instead of swords.

15 1st Madras Native Infantry, the Corps of Madras Pioneers; set 67. This is the bulkier Indian infantry figure introduced about 1913. The longer tunic no longer has a panel of facing colour and no equipment is worn (except a waist belt). This and the following sets, which were available until 1940, did not usually contain an officer.

16 2nd Bombay Native Infantry, later 4th Bombay Grenadiers; set 68. The post-1913 figure, still with the incorrect blue tunic; see (13).
17 7th Bengal Infantry, later 3rd Battalion 7th Rajputs. This figure, very similar to (15) but with yellow facings (just visible on this battered example), replaced the earlier type in set 64; see (14). From 1934-40 the 3rd Battalion 7th Rajputs were available in the separate eight-piece set 1342.
18 The 12th Frontier Force Regiment, 3rd Battalion Sikhs, later the 53rd Sikhs Frontier Force; set 1621. This figure is surprisingly attractive in his drab uniform with dark blue facings; sadly he lacks the Sikh beard of the earlier casting! The set of eight was only available from

1938-40, and it is quite rare.
19 Gurkha Rifles, 1st King George's Own (The Malaun Regiment); set 197. Introduced in 1919, and available after the war until 1959, this is an attractive little figure of a Gurkha marching at the trail in dark green, with his kukri at the back of his waist belt.
20,23 Indian Infantry Marching at the Trail; set 1892. This interesting set, available briefly in 1940-41, saw a revival of the pre-World War I infantryman, now in khaki (20), with the new British battledress officer from set 1858 (23). It is rare as a boxed set, and most khaki Indians found are likely to be from set 1893.
20-23 Royal Indian Army Service Corps, with Officer and Mule; set 1893. First produced in 1940, this

seven-piece set was available again after the war until 1959. It comprised one battledress officer (23), one empty-handed mule handler (22), one mule from the Mountain Artillery (21) and four Indian infantry at the trail (20).
24 This scarce figure, which uses the Indian cavalryman in a greenish khaki, with lighter turban and cummerbund, and the post-war sword at the carry, is probably from the very rare 12-piece set 2013: Indian Army Mounted. A similar figure would have been used as the officer in the very rare set 1903: Indian Army Mountain Battery. It used the gun and mules from set 28: Mountain Artillery — see *inset* on *page 47* — with six of the Indian mule handlers (22).

Inset (above): *On the left is a very unusual medical orderly, based on the first-version RAF airman from set 240 (centre), but in khaki uniform with a Red Cross emblem on the left arm, a brown belt and white gloves. This figure is possibly from a special khaki version of the large RAMC display set 1300. On the right is the quite scarce military policeman, only available in the station set 1R from 1954-59.*

Britains' first portrayal of army medical personnel came in 1905 with the 24-piece set 137. This contained one Senior Medical Officer (1), two doctors (2), three pairs of stretcher bearers with stretchers (5-6), and eight wounded men; two with arms in slings (7), three with bandaged heads (8), and three with hands behind heads (9).

1 Senior Medical Officer; he stands in a relaxed pose in a dark blue uniform, with a general's pattern cocked hat with falling plumes.
2 The doctor wears the same uniform as (1), but with a ball-topped helmet. Note that (1) and (2) remained round-based throughout production.
3-4 Nurses, first version. These small nurses wear red capes and white aprons over grey floor-length dresses.
5-6 Stretcher bearers. The first stretcher bearers had oval bases; these are square-based but still with gaiters. Their uniform is dark blue with red facings, with a ball-topped helmet of which two versions are shown here, (6) being the earlier pattern.
7-9 Wounded soldiers; (7) has his right arm in a sling, with his jacket open to reveal his grey shirt, and a white helmet on the back of his head; (8) has a bandaged head, and appears to lie at attention; while (9), although with a bandaged left leg, seems far more relaxed — his hands are behind his head and his helmet is tipped forward over his eyes.
10-11 Stretcher bearers, 1930s. During this period the stretcher bearers lost their gaiters and became straight-trousered, this version remaining until the end of production in 1940.
12 Nurse, second version, 1930s. A taller figure with a wide white head-dress, white apron, red cape and grey dress, with black-stockinged legs now visible. Included in a number of sets, this nurse was available up to 1961 in set 1723, with battledress stretcher bearers.
13 An unusual and attractive good second-grade nurse in a blue cape and dress. Not listed, and presumably for sale singly, this may be a navy or air force nurse.
14 RAMC nurse; no. 122P. A rather basic second-grade painting of the nurse from the New Crown range, first issued in 1956.
15-16 Stretcher Party Unit of the Royal Army Medical Corps, Steel Helmets; set 1719. Available in 1939-40, rapidly being replaced by the more up-to-date battledress figures, these men in

service dress and steel helmets replaced the same figures in peaked caps.

17-18 Casualties. The figure on the stretcher, and the one in the tent, are both castings of a civilian casualty. He is straight-trousered with an open-necked jacket with shirt and tie underneath, but painted khaki. The figure which probably should go with (15-16) is shown at (24) painted as a wounded civilian!

19-21 Stretcher bearers, battledress. These were available concurrently with the service dress figures just before World War II, and were available in set 1723 and others until 1961. The wounded man with his arm in a sling (21) is an interesting re-working of (7) with a bandaged

head and a map pocket on his trousers, which are straight rather than gaitered.

22-24 Air Raid Precautions Stretcher Squad; set 1759. This grim set, portraying one of the horrors of war which happily did not materialize, contained two stretcher bearer teams, and a man leaning forward with a gas detector stick (not shown). All except the casualties wear black anti-gas suits and respirators. The civilian casualty is a repainting of (8), complete with gaiters.

25 Military Policeman. This figure talking to the ambulance driver is actually from a post-war railway set no. 1R (see also *Inset*).

26 Royal Army Medical Corps, With Ambulance Wagon; set 145. The splendid horse-drawn ambulance

in review order was introduced in 1906, the example shown being the same except for the later breast harness on the horses, which replaced collar harness in about 1925. The basic vehicle was the same as the more common no. 146 General Service Wagon, but with a cloth tilt supported on wires, and an extra pair of horses. This set had a brief revival from 1954-59. From 1919-40 a khaki version was available numbered 145A, later 145O, the men being in khaki uniforms with peaked caps.

27 Army Ambulance, with Driver, Wounded and Stretcher; set 1512. Britain's first motor ambulance, introduced in 1937, using the cab, bonnet and chassis of the series of lorries known as

"square radiator type", first available in 1934. The van-type body is made of tinplate. Note that this and the later model both have reversed colour roundels, suggesting Swiss markings rather than red crosses!

28 Ambulance; set 1512. The post-war vehicle with a round-nosed radiator and a more streamlined look. On this model, produced from 1946-56, the driver's door opens. The final version produced from 1957-60 had a new cab unit without opening doors, a split windscreen, and a fixed driver in a beret with movable arms.

29 A small Red Cross tent, on a wire frame, of unknown make.

30 "Royal Seamless" tent; from a range of 20 different shapes and sizes listed by Britains.

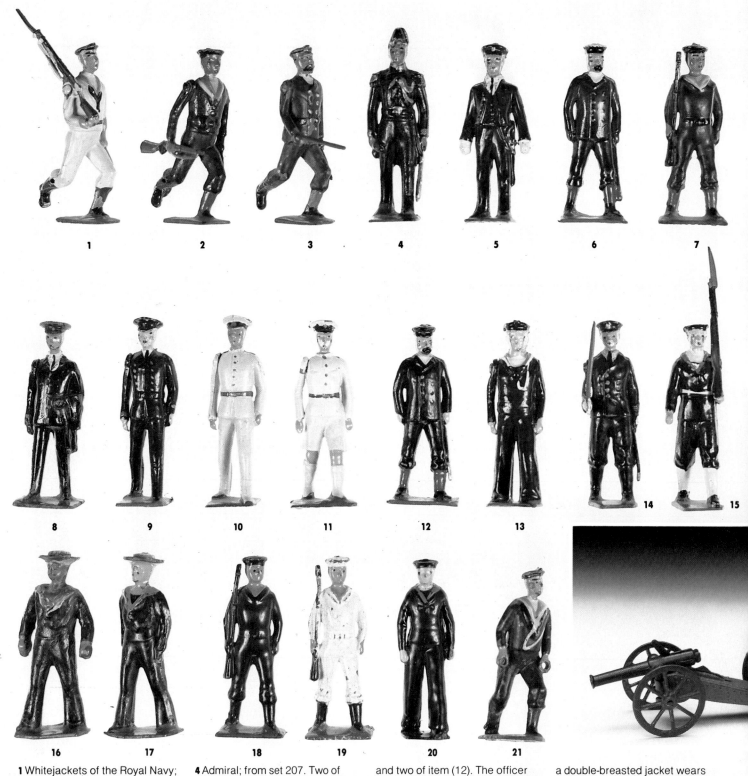

1   2   3   4   5   6   7

8   9   10   11   12   13   14   15

16   17   18   19   20   21

1 Whitejackets of the Royal Navy; set 80. An early-version sailor with rifle at the slope, from a set of eight which included a petty officer (3), produced from 1897-1940. Later variations have square bases, larger heads, and rifles carried at the trail.

2 Bluejackets of the Royal Navy; set 78. This set has the same history as set 80, although rifles at the trail were carried throughout. This is a later figure with square base, larger head, and a rifle without a magazine.

3 "Petty officer" running with sword extended; used with sets 78, 79 (*inset*) and 80. Although usually referred to as a petty officer, his buttons, in two rows of four rather than two rows of three, are correct for an officer.

4 Admiral; from set 207. Two of these officers were available from 1923-40 in an eight-piece set of Officers and Petty Officers of the Royal Navy.

5 Midshipman; set 207. He wears a short pea-jacket and an Eton collar, and carries a naval dirk.

6-7 Royal Naval Reserve; set 151. From its inception in 1907 to 1940 this was always a square-based set, with fixed-arm sailors (7) at the shoulder arms. A rare early version of the officer (6) with a movable right arm also exists.

8-12 Officers and Petty Officers of the Royal Navy, in Blue Uniforms, and in White Uniforms; set 1911. Produced in 1940, and post-war until 1959, this seven-piece set contained one of item (8), two of item (9), one each of (10) and (11)

and two of item (12). The officer with overcoat (8) is based on the yachtsman from set 168. (9) is the least satisfactory figure; it uses the US Marine casting shown at (2) *page 80*, and the white shirt, tie and double row of buttons are painted over a closed collar and single-breasted tunic. In contrast the same casting as used for (10) works quite well. The officer in shorts (11) uses the second-version scout-master casting. The petty officer (12) uses the pre-war RNVR casting, but with a blue-topped cap and green gaiters.

13 British Sailors, Regulation Dress; set 1510. An eight-piece set without an officer, produced in 1937-40 and 1946-59.

14-15 Royal Navy, Marching at the Slope; set 2080. The officer (14) in

a double-breasted jacket wears black leather gaiters, while the sailor (15) wears regulation dress with the white web belt and long gaiters. Available from 1953-61.

16-17 These rather Victorian-looking sailors in straw hats, with fixed arms and hexagonal bases, were for sale singly from the 1920s to 1940. There are two versions: the earlier, no. 26C with the arms away from the body (16), and a later one, no. 19N, with the arms close to the body (17).

18 Royal Navy Bluejacket; no. 49N. A simple second-grade painting of the RNVR figure.

19 Royal Navy Whitejacket; no. 50N. A second-grade painting.

20 British Bluejacket; no. 116P in the post-war New Crown range, and in set 1081A pre-war.

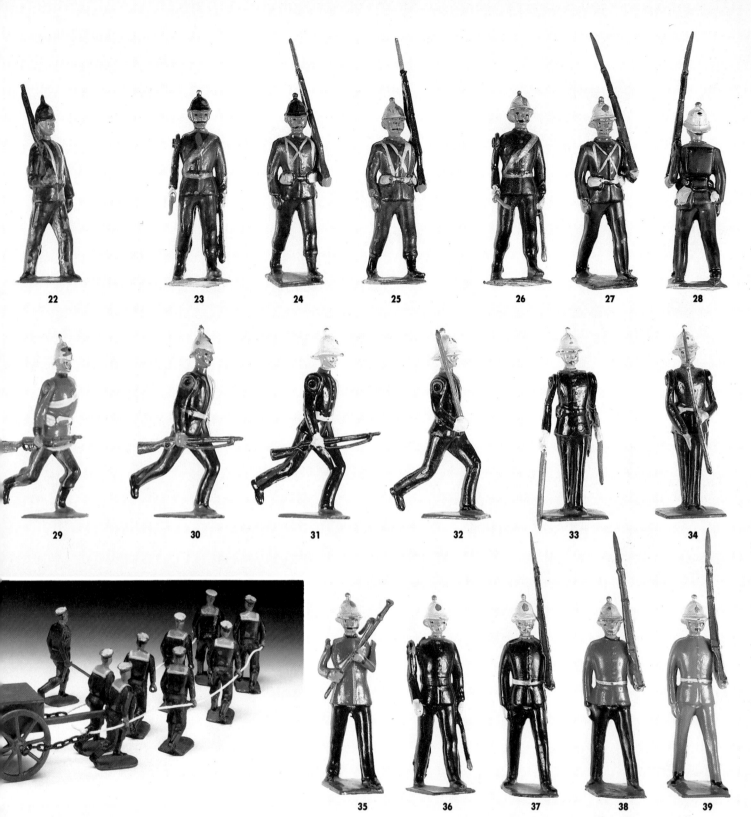

22 23 24 25 26 27 28

29 30 31 32 33 34

35 36 37 38 39

Inset(above): *Royal Navy Landing Party with Limber and Gun; set 79. In this attractive set, eight sailors (21) led by an officer (3) haul a gun and a small limber with an opening hinged lid. It was available from 1897-1940, and post-war from 1952-63.*

21 Sailor, Royal Navy Landing Party with Gun; set 79 (see *inset*).
22 Royal Marine Artilleryman; a second-grade painting from the ''X'' series, using the 1895-1910 Royal Sussex figure shown at (2) *page 50*. Until 1922 the marines were divided into Royal Marine Artillery, in blue uniforms, and Royal Marine Light Infantry who wore infantry-style uniforms. From 1905 both branches adopted the white foreign service

helmet for home service use.
23-24 Royal Marine Artillery; set 35. This officer (23) and man (24) are the third version with square bases and gaiters, *c*1908.
25 Royal Marine Artillery; set 35. The same figure from a year or two later, now with a white helmet.
26 Royal Marine officer; set 35. Still gaitered, and with an artillery-type gold cross-belt, this officer has the larger marine-pattern helmet introduced *c*1928.
27-28 Royal Marines; set 35. Front and back views of the Royal Marine produced from 1930-36 which, like the fusiliers at (34-35) *page 51*, became straight-trousered but kept the pack and full equipment.
29 Royal Marine Light Infantry; set 97. This set of seven men and an

officer, using the same casting with an extended sword arm, was introduced in 1899. It used the same figure as the York and Lancaster Regiment shown at (25-27) *page 51*.
30 Royal Marines, Running at the Trail; set 97. An early running marine, produced after the change of set title from RMLI but still with the infantry-type helmet.
31-32 Royal Marines, Marching at the Slope and Running at the Trail, with Officers; set 1284. This set, containing eight of each type, was produced from 1933-61 with the usual break. These figures differ from the pre-war marines in set 97 only by slight differences in painting style, and the officer's sword (32) at the carry.
33-34 Royal Marines Presenting

Arms; set 2071. From the seven-piece set available from 1953-60.
35 Band of the Royal Marine Light Infantry; set 1622. An example of a musician from the rare and colourful 21-piece band only available from 1938-40.
36-37 Royal Marines Marching at the Slope; set 35. This set adopted the standard 1910 marching figure rather than the fusilier-type body in 1937.
38 Royal Marine Light Infantry at the Slope; set 1620. This is a rare retrospective figure, in effect the 1936 Royal Marine in a scarlet jacket, only available from 1938-40.
39 Royal Marines at the Slope in Tropical Dress; set 1619. Like (38) but in a pale khaki uniform with white helmet, this rare figure was only available from 1938-40.

1 Britains monoplane: no. 433. A slightly battered example of a rare piece. The fuselage is hollow-cast with tinplate wings and tail, and detachable pilot.

2 Walking pilot. This figure giving a "thumbs up" sign is of unknown make, but similar in style to the pilot by Cresent (9).

3 Pilot in Sidcot suit; a Britains second-grade figure, similar to (37) but with a fixed arm.

4-6 RAF figures from the 1950s, by Crescent. (4) is a pilot in peaked cap and windcheater with map case, while (5) is a RAF Regiment figure marching at the slope; these are both rather undersized. (6) is the science-fiction hero Dan Dare, usually in pale green but here, with "50 mission hat" and medals, in RAF service!

7 Airman in battledress, by Johillco. This figure with a steel helmet slung at his hip is more usually found as a soldier in khaki.

8 WAAF (Womens Auxilliary Air Force) by Johillco.

9 Pilot in flying suit holding a map case; Crescent no. B185.

10 Ground crew with petrol can; Crescent no. A83.

11 RAF airman in service dress, of unknown make.

12 Airman by Crescent, quaintly listed as "A81: RAF Infantry".

13 Airman in service dress; from Britains 22-piece set 2011, 1948-59, which contained nearly all the RAF figures.

14 World War I style pilot. This tall figure was available in a boxed set from Crescent in 1948.

15 A solid World War I pilot made from a home-cast mould of (25).

16-17 Officer and man, from Britains set 240: Royal Air Force, produced from 1925-40. These attractive movable-arm empty-handed figures wear the uniform of the early RAF.

18 A pilot in full flying kit, by the US firm Moulded Miniatures.

19-21 RAF Regiment, by Britains. These were only available in Display Set 2011 and as individual pieces in Picture Packs. Set 2011 included: one officer (19), a Bren gunner (21) and six men with slung rifles (20).

22 Airman in peaked cap holding a swagger stick, by Crescent.

23 Fire-fighter of the Royal Air Force, by Britains. A set of eight, no. 1758, was issued in 1939-40, and two were included in set 2011.

Left: *The Timpo Airport. A rare but remarkably crude set of airfield buildings by Timpo, believed to be for export! The upper two buildings, of fibreboard nailed together, are freestanding. Note that the four pilots made of resin are only about 20mm (0.78in) high, and in turn dwarf the two diecast B17 bombers.*

24 RAF pilot; Johillco 267PC. This is really a World War I figure in a heavy leather overcoat.

25 A pilot in World War I style leather jacket and breeches, but painted dark RAF blue; probably by Taylor and Barrett.

26 RAF rigger; Johillco 267RC.

27 RAF mechanic; Johillco 267MC. Both (26) and (27) were probably designed as RFC men.

28 World War II pilot, by Johillco.

29 The same as (28) but in white.

30-31 These odd figures are based on the Crescent airmen in jacket and in greatcoat, but have German-style helmets. Possibly they are meant to be Luftwaffe.

32 RAF airman in overcoat; Crescent A82. Note the similarity to Britains figure (33).

33 RAF airman in greatcoat, by Britains, available in set 2011, based on set 331: US Army Air Force Officers in Overcoats.

34-35 Pilots running to their planes, by Johillco.

36 RAF pilot in full flying kit, by Britains. Available in 1940-41 in set 1894, and set 1906 with ground staff and fire fighters. After the war two pilots were included in set 2011 and were

also available as a Picture Pack.

37 Pilot in Sidcot suit, from Britains set 2011.

38 RAF officer in battledress with document; Britains set 2011. This was based on the Home Guard shown at (25) *page 85.*

39 RAF despatch rider, by Britains, only available in set 2011.

40-41 Royal Air Force Marching at the Slope with Officer; Britains set 2073. These figures are from an eight-piece set produced from 1953, in time for the coronation of Elizabeth II, until 1959. The officer (40) uses the same casting as the man, but with a sheathed sword in the left hand.

42 RAF Commodore; Britains Picture Pack 1081B. Like the naval officer at (8) *page 62,* this figure uses the civilian yachtsman casting.

43 WAAF by Britains. Two WAAFs were included with the pilots (36) in set 1894 before the war. Post-war, as a WRAF (Womens Royal Air Force), she was available in a Picture Pack, and in set 2011.

44 Band of the RAF; set 1527. This attractive 12-piece band (the fife player is missing from this example) used the same figures and instrumentation as set 1290: Khaki Band, and set 1301: US Band. Available from 1937-40 and intermittently post-war.

45 Aeroplane by Mignot. From a display set first produced *c*1920, this aircraft is from a limited re-issue produced in 1983.

46 A very basic RAF airfield layout by an unknown maker; 1940s.

47 A tinplate biplane fighter by the Italian firm of Ingap, *c*1938.

Britains produced an extensive range of troops of foreign armies. Some commemorated recent events and conflicts, while others reflected a growing export market to a particular country. In the next few pages the troops of some 25 different states are illustrated, in alphabetical order, followed by sections on Canada and the USA.

1 Bodyguard of the Emperor of Abyssinia, at Attention; set 1424. When Italy invaded Abyssinia Britains were quick to produce figures of the combatants. This fixed-arm figure (1) from a box of eight without an officer wears a brown-topped peaked cap, a light green uniform with epaulettes and an aiguillette, a "Sam Browne" belt with a rather flimsy

sheathed sword, breeches, puttees and bare feet. Available 1936-40 and briefly from 1948-49.
2 Abyssinian Tribesmen, Slope Arms; set 1425. This interesting figure is a re-working of that used in set 187: Arabs on Foot, shown at (14) *page 88*, but bare-headed with a fixed arm. Also introduced in 1936, this set lasted until 1959.
3 Argentine Cadets, Military School; set 219. This attractive figure, although rather bulky for a cadet, wears a Prussian-style plumed helmet and blue-grey tunic with frogging over white trousers. Note the distinctive rifle arm that Britains used for Spanish and South American troops, with the rifle butt brought across in front of the body.
4 Argentine Infantry; set 216.

These figures, without an officer, wear a blue-grey Napoleonic style full-dress uniform of shako and tail-coat — worn to this day by some Argentinian units. Produced 1925-40 and 1946-49.
5-6 Argentine Infantry, Steel Helmets; set 1837. These very rare figures in khaki with sand-coloured helmets use the German body casting with the rimless Italian steel helmet, a combination also found in the rare Netherlands and Polish Infantry shown at (11-13) *page 74*. Issued briefly at the beginning of World War II, it has been suggested that the Argentinians were produced as an expedient to use up castings which would have been issued as soldiers of Poland or the Netherlands, had these

countries not fallen to the Nazis.
7 Argentine Military Cadets; set 1836. A slightly battered example of a rare figure, introduced at the same time as the Argentine infantry in khaki, but also available in 1948-49. This set, which replaced the more picturesque figures of set 219 (3), used the standard marching infantry figures, but with peaked caps, and included an officer marching with sheathed sword. Set 1835, the Argentine Naval Cadets, produced at the same time and also rare, used the same castings in dark blue with white-topped caps and no facings.
8-9 Argentine Cavalry; set 217. These splendid figures use a horse and rider casting that is shared only with the Uruguayan

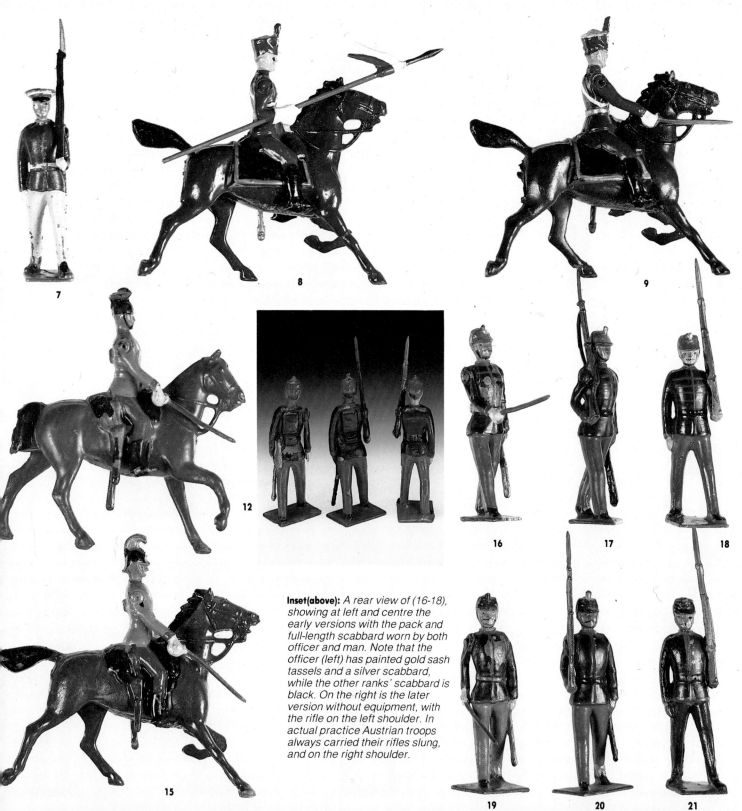

7

8

9

12

16

17

18

15

Inset(above): *A rear view of (16-18), showing at left and centre the early versions with the pack and full-length scabbard worn by both officer and man. Note that the officer (left) has painted gold sash tassels and a silver scabbard, while the other ranks' scabbard is black. On the right is the later version without equipment, with the rifle on the left shoulder. In actual practice Austrian troops always carried their rifles slung, and on the right shoulder.*

19

20

21

cavalry, shown at (23-24) *pages 74-75.* They wear grey-blue uniforms with yellow-topped shakoes, red plumes, collars and epaulettes. The men have lances with pennants in the Argentine colours of white and blue, while the officer has an extended sword arm. It was a five-piece set from 1925-47, then four-piece to 1959.
10-12 Austro-Hungarian Lancers; set 175. Unusually, Britains Austrian cavalry contained both an officer and a trumpeter in the five-piece set. These simple but attractive lancers ride the ''Scots Grey'' walking horse; note that their lancer caps are taller and slighter than those of the British, with smaller plumes and no cap lines. The officer has an extended sword arm while the trooper has a

sword at the carry, not a lance. The trumpeter rides a grey horse. Introduced in 1912, these now uncommon figures were produced until 1940.
13-15 Austro-Hungarian Dragoons; set 176. The other set of Austrian cavalry, also available from 1912-40, featured dragoons mounted on trotting horses, with a trumpeter on a grey. Apart from their distinctive ''classical'' helmets, they wear much the same uniform as the lancers: light blue-grey tunics with red facings and breeches. Like the lancers, this is a desirable set.
16-18 Austro-Hungarian Infantry of the Line; set 177. There has been some doubt as to whether these figures, or those at (19-21) were intended by Britains to represent

Austrian line infantry, as the latter are a far better representation of a line regiment. Britains would appear to have been a little confused, as the colourful uniform shown here seems to be based on that of a Hungarian ''Honved'' or territorial unit. When introduced in 1912 the set used an unusual figure with full equipment marching diagonally across a square base. This was also used for the early Prussian officer shown at (3) *page 72.* Later the set used the standard 1910 infantry figure. (16) is the early-type officer with extended sword arm; (17) is the early-version man with a ''droopy sling'' rifle on the right shoulder, while (18) is an example of the later type without equipment, and with the rifle at

the slope on the left shoulder, dating from the 1930s. The set was deleted from the Britains catalogue in 1940.
19-21 Austro-Hungarian Foot Guards; set 178. These figures use the same castings as set 177, and in fact are a quite good portrayal of Austrian line infantry. In the Austrian Army the only foot guards were a guard battalion formed from members of other regiments, who wore a dark green uniform and falling plume helmet, similar to (3). The later version of this set (21) should not be confused with set 166: Italian Infantry, shown at (18-19) *page 72* which used the same casting but painted as though with a double-breasted tunic, and with a red top to the headgear.

1-2 Belgian Cavalry, Review Order (2me Chasseurs à Cheval); set 190. Belgium, as an ally of the UK, was well represented in the Britains range. The cavalry trooper (1) sits a standing horse first used for the French Dragons in 1905 — see (11) *page 70*. The men carry carbines; the officer, with extended sword arm, rides a cantering grey like that ridden by the French cavalry officers. They were available from 1913-40, and from 1948-59.

3 Belgian Infantry, Review Order; set 189. This set contained eight men at the ready with fixed bayonets, dressed in French-style uniforms with dark blue greatcoats, but with light blue-grey trousers. It was produced from 1913-40.

4-7 Belgian Infantry, Service Dress, Steel Helmets, Firing in Standing, Kneeling and Lying Positions, with Machine-gunners; set 1383. This set, with its very full title, had three men in each firing position and two machine-gunners, just like the set on which it was based — no. 215: French Infantry in Action, shown at (7-10) *page 71*. From 1934-40 they were in a brown khaki like (8-9), but post-war figures, such as these, wear green khaki. The set was available until 1960.

8-9 Belgian Infantry (Service Order at the Slope); set 1389. Available from 1934-40, this set used the French infantry in shrapnel-proof helmets shown at (6) *page 71*, but in khaki uniform. Unlike the French troops, this set had an

officer (9) based on the German officer casting, but with a French ''Adrian'' pattern helmet.

10 Belgian Grenadiers Marching at the Slope, with Officer; set 2009. The new Belgian figures produced after World War II (10-12) were curiously outdated, wearing as they did the uniforms of the 1900s. The Belgian grenadier (10) uses the body and arm casting of the French infantryman in steel helmet, no. 192, but with a British fusilier head. The officer uses the British Guards officer casting — see (11) *page 48* — but with a British fusilier head. This set was available from 1948-59.

11 Belgian Chasseur à Pied; no. 133P. Sadly this rather attractive figure of a charging Belgian light

infantryman was only available in this very second-grade paint finish, issued in the New Crown range as late as 1956. The basic casting is that of the Japanese infantryman — see (1) *page 74*. Although still round-based, this was modified by having the trousers filled out, and equipped with a plumed kepi.

12 Belgian Grenadier; no. 132P. This must have a strong claim to being the worst figure Britains ever produced! It is the second-grade fixed-arm no. 41P Guardsman from the New Crown range, denied even a scarlet jacket and blue trousers, but turned out in basic black with splashes of red on the shoulders.

13 Bulgarian Infantry; set 172. One of a group of sets produced in

13

14

15

16

17

18   19   20   21   22   23   24

1911, representing the troops of the Balkan War and now all highly collectable. This Bulgarian infantryman at the trail employs the body casting first used for set 133: Russian Infantry — see (1-2) *page 76* — but with a smaller-crowned white cap with a peak and a light blue band. An officer used the same figure but with an extended sword arm. The set was discontinued in 1940.

14 Chinese Infantry; set 241. When Britains produced this set in 1925 they chose to portray a sword-wielding "Boxer" of 1900, rather than a contemporary Chinese infantryman. The set contained eight of the same figure, in yellow or green mandarin hats and red, green or blue loose tunics over white trousers and black boots.

The set was discontinued in 1940 and is fairly rare.

15-17 Danish Guard Hussar Regiment; set 2018. This set of magnificent Danish hussars used the old Prussian hussar casting — see (5-6) *pages 72-73* — but with a different head and without the carbine. Unusually the set contained eight pieces: an officer (15) and six troopers (17) on brown horses, and a trumpeter on a grey. The difference between the troopers and officer, who all hold swords at the carry, is the silver trim on the officer's uniform and saddlecloth. The set was only available from 1955-59, so it is now quite rare.

18-19 Danish Livgarde, Marching with Officer; set 2019. This attractive set of seven pieces

uses a unique casting for the Danish footguard figure (19), which has a red tunic with white cross-belts, and a rifle cradled in both arms which plug in at the shoulders. The black bearskin cap has a red patch at the back. The officer (18) uses the standard marching officer body, but with the head of the Yeoman of the Guard captain — see (3) *page 90*.

20 Danish Hussar and Life Guards: set 2135. A short-lived "half set" only available from 1957-59, teamed a hussar (17) with two Life Guards. The only distinguishing feature of the latter is the blue patch on the bearskin cap shown in this back view, rather than the red used in (18-19).

21-22 Irish Free State Infantry; set 1603. The first-version Irish

infantryman (22) uses the German infantry casting shown at (8) *page 73* to good effect, with a peaked cap, dark grey-green uniform, and brown belt and boots. The officer (21) uses the fixed-arm US officer casting — see (13) *page 78*. This version was available from 1937-40 and then 1948-49.

23-24 Republic of Ireland, Infantry Battle Order; set 1603. In 1950 a new Irish infantryman (24) was introduced, this time using the US infantry figure shown at (28-30) *page 79*, but with a British steel helmet and a rifle at the trail. The officer (23), is in a lighter green tunic open at the collar, and light green-grey breeches, and has a plain movable right arm. Discontinued in 1959, both versions of this set are scarce.

1-2 Infanterie de Ligne; set 141. Both the officer (2) and man (1) of the line infantry are first-version figures, clearly stamped 9.5.1905 on their oval bases.

3 This excellent French line infantryman, in "grande tenue" or parade dress of a tunic and a kepi with pom-pom — but still with pouches and pack — was only available from the Paris Office.

4 Zouaves; set 142. This splendid figure of a French North African soldier at the charge, in turbaned fez, open short jacket and baggy trousers, was to have a long life from 1905 right through to 1966. The marching officer (2) was included in the first eight-piece set of round-based figures, but this was soon dropped in favour of another charging man. In 1954

a mounted officer (23) replaced two of the men.

5 Turcos; set 191. This set uses the same figure as the Zouaves, but in pale blue with yellow trim. Introduced in 1913, it was discontinued in 1940, and was only available post-war from 1957-59 in a rare "half set" containing two Turcos and a mounted officer (23). Turcos, so-called because of their Turkish style dress, were more properly the Tirailleur Algeriens, or Algerian sharpshooters.

6 Infanterie de Ligne (Shrapnel-proof Helmets); set 192. This figure, depicting the new horizon blue uniform and "Adrian" steel helmet introduced in 1915, is based on the early infantry of the line casting, with a modified pack

and a new head. It was available from c1916-40.

7-10 Infanterie Firing, Standing, Kneeling and Lying, and Machine-gunners; set 215. This fine 14-piece set of French infantrymen in action, introduced in 1924, contained four each of items (7), (8) and (9), and two machine-gunners.

11 Dragons; set 140. The French cavalry sets introduced in 1905 used modified versions of the existing cavalry horses, with bulky saddle-bags and blanket rolls on the saddlery, and fuller breeches and boots on the mounted figures. The Dragons (dragoons) are armed with lances (the tip is missing from this example), and early versions have a separate carbine which clips

into the back of the rider's body and is held in place by the falling plume. The officer, as for all the French cavalry, uses the cantering horse (23) in grey. The rarest of the French cavalry, they were not available after 1940.

12 Cuirassiers; set 138. The French heavy cavalry, in breastplates and helmets with flowing plumes, ride walking "Scots Grey" type horses and are armed with swords. The commonest of the French cavalry figures, they were available right through to 1966.

13-14 Infanterie de Ligne; set 141. The later square-based gaitered French line infantryman (13), in an almost grey rather than blue greatcoat and red kepi, replaced (1) and remained in production alongside the horizon blue figures

in steel helmets. See also (27).
The rather attractive movable-
arm officer (14) replaced the
fixed-arm officer (2) for a while,
until being dropped altogether.
15,22 French Foreign Legion
Marching at the Slope, with
Mounted Officer; set 1711. This
set, available from 1939-40 and
then from 1948-66, was perhaps
inspired by Hollywood. The
infantryman from set 141 (13) was
used, but with a white-topped kepi
and, oddly, white cuffs.
16-20 French Foreign Legion,
Firing and Charging with Officer and
Machine-gunner; set 2095. This
14-piece set used the body
castings from set 215 (7-10), with
kepis instead of steel helmets, but
with two additions. One of the
machine-gunners was replaced

by a kneeling officer with a pair of
binoculars, and two of the
kneeling figures were replaced by
two charging legionnaires which
were revived from a much earlier
Paris Office figure.
21 Chasseurs à Cheval; set 139.
These attractive cavalry in
plumed shakoes and tunics with
black frogging were introduced in
1905. They carry carbines, and
are mounted on trotting horses;
the officer rides a cantering grey.
22 French Foreign Legion officer,
mounted at the halt. This empty-
handed figure, mounted on the
standing horse used for the
Dragons, was included in the set
of marching legionnaires (15) and
late sets of the Foreign Legion in
action (16-20); it was also
available as a Picture Pack.

23 Zouave officer. With the
appropriate head and paint finish
this figure on a cantering horse
has served as the officer for all
the French cavalry. In 1954 he
replaced two of the charging
Zouaves in set 142; in the rare
"half set" no. 2138 he led two
Turcos into action, but in Picture
Pack 1329B he was a Foreign
Legion officer — a most varied
military career.
24-25 Matelots; set 143. Based on
the running British sailors, but
with a French sailor's cap with
red pom-pom, all versions of this
set are very rare. The first, 1905
version (24) carries a Lebel rifle at
the slope (the bayonet missing
from this example), but this was
soon changed to the standard
Britains arm with rifle at the trail.

(25) is from the brief post-war
revival of this set.
26 Troops of the Algerian Spahis; set
2172. A rare late set of French
Colonial cavalry troopers on grey
horses, of unique design. A
standard bearer rode a brown
horse. A five-piece set, it was only
produced from 1958-60.
27 Infanterie de Ligne; set 141. In
late examples of this set the kepi
is finished in a medium blue,
representing the cloth cover that
the French troops wore in 1914. It
was available until 1940.
28 French Foreign Legion Officer;
Picture Pack 1367B. This figure
was only available post-war in a
Picture Pack. Previously, with a
pom-pom on his kepi, this officer
had accompanied the Paris Office
infantry in parade dress (3).

1-4 Prussian Infantry of the Line; set 154. Produced from 1908-40, both versions shown seem to have been available more or less concurrently. Figures (1-2) use the fusilier body with Slade Wallace equipment and gaiters. The officer (1) is distinguished from the men by having a drawn sword in his left hand. Figures (3-4) march diagonally across their bases with the right foot forward like the Austrian troops shown at (16-17) *page 67*, and in fact the officer (3) uses the same pattern body. The infantryman (4) is a well detailed figure with the correct pattern pack and equipment. All are finished in dark blue tunics with red facings, and trousers in dark green rather than the slate grey worn in reality.

5-6 Prussian Hussars; set 153. Britains' only set of German cavalry, these unique figures, later adapted for the Danish hussars shown at (15-17) *page 69*, wear the red tunic and dark blue pelisse (a fur-trimmed jacket worn hanging nonchalantly from the left shoulder) of the Prussian Guard Hussars. All ranks ride cantering horses, with carbines suspended at the hip; the officer (6) has an incorrect replacement arm — he should have the ''Continental'' type sword at the carry, tucked close into the body. Produced 1908-40, this is a rare and sought-after set.

7-10 German Infantry with Officer (Active Service Dress); set 432. Introduced in 1931, this figure gives a good overall impression of a steel-helmeted German infantryman in a patch-pocket tunic, breeches and jackboots. The first-version figures produced up to 1940 (7-8) wear all-grey uniforms. Available post-war right up to 1966, the same figures were turned out in dark green helmets and tunics with blue-grey breeches (9-10).

11 Pilots of the German Luftwaffe (Full Flying Kit); set 1895. This set contained eight walking German Air Force pilots using the same casting as set 1894: RAF Pilots — see (36) *page 65* — but in grey flying suits with black equipment. They were only available in 1940-41 and are rare.

12-13 Greek Infantry; set 171. This was one of the group of ''Balkan'' sets produced in 1911. This first-version Greek infantryman (12) uses the gaitered running at the trail figure with a small peaked cap, in a tobacco brown uniform with a yellow cap band. The officer used the same figure with an extended sword arm. The later 1930s version (13) uses the full-trousered figure in a greenish khaki painting. It was produced from 1911-40 and is quite scarce.

14-15 Greek Cavalry: set 170. These attractive and rare figures use standard British Cavalry type castings but with small-crowned peaked caps like the Greek infantry. The uniform is dark green with white frogging and cap band and red collar and cuffs. They were produced from 1911-40.

16-17 Greek Evzones; set 196. These figures depict the Greek Light

Infantry, who became the Royal Guards, in their distinctive uniform based on Greek national costume, including the "fustanella" or pleated kilt-like garment. They are among the few Britains figures to step off on the right foot. Strangely, from the set's introduction in 1919 until 1940 the Evzones were incorrectly painted with an all-red jacket and brown boots exposing bare knees in a very dark skin colour (16). Post-war they were correctly painted with a black waistcoat over a basically white costume topped by a small red cap (17). The set, which never had an officer, lasted until 1966.

18-19 Italian Infantry (Review Order); set 166. This set, introduced in 1911, used the same casting as

the later Austrians — see (21) *page 67* — and could indeed be confused with the foot guard. The Italians have rifles without fixed bayonets, and are painted as though they have double-breasted tunics, which is correct for an officer, when included, but wrong for an infantryman. The officer (18) has a white-topped shako, the man (19) a red-topped shako.

20-21 Italian Cavalry; set 165. These attractive figures use the standing horse first used for the French Dragons — see (11) *page 70*. Their headgear is the Paris Office French officer's kepi with pom-pom, painted white to represent an Italian lancer's fur cap with a cloth cover. The officer has a drawn sword arm (21) while the men have lances which are

topped with blue pennants (20).
22 Italian Infantry with Shrapnel-proof Helmets; set 1435. The Italian invasion of Abyssinia in 1935 inspired the production of a second batch of Italian figures in 1936, including this infantryman — a really good up-to-date portrayal in a grey-green rimless steel helmet, an open-necked tunic and baggy trousers. Unfortunately without an officer, this set was available until 1959.
23 Italian Infantry, Colonial Service Dress; set 1436. Dressed for Abyssinia, this interesting figure uses the same casting as (22), but topped with a broad tropical helmet, and finished in yellow ochre. This set did not reappear post-war, and is scarce.
24 Italian Bersaglieri; set 169. This

set of Italian light infantry was introduced in 1911, at the same time as the infantry and cavalry. A fixed-arm figure with a slung rifle, wearing the distinctive broad-brimmed hat, he marches off on the right foot. The set was available intermittently after the war, when an officer was sometimes included, similar to (18) but empty-handed, with dark blue trousers, and out of step.
25-26 Italian Carabinieri; set 1437, available 1936-40 and 1954-59. The splendid marching Carabinieri (26), in the ceremonial full dress they wear to this day. Post-war an officer (25) in a relaxed pose, using the casting of the Yeoman of the Guard captain — see (3) *page 90* — was included in the set.

73

1   **2**   **3**   **4**

11   **12**   **13**   **14**   **15**

21   **22**   **23**

1 Japanese Infantry; set 134. Introduced in 1904 at the time of the Russo-Japanese war, this set of eight charging figures never had an officer, and remained round-based right through to 1940. Oddly, although it is otherwise quite an accurate figure Britains nearly always painted this and the Japanese cavalry (2) in light blue tunics, rather than the correct dark blue.

2 Japanese Cavalry Officers; set 135. This officer rides a trotting horse, but the troopers in set 135 ride the head-down cantering horses and carry carbines; all wear light blue. Produced from 1904-40, and scarce.

3 A rare Japanese infantryman from a late version of set 134, correctly attired in dark blue.

4-5 Mexican Infantry; set 186 — or "Los Rurales de La Federacion (Mexico's Pride)" as they were rather floridly described on the box lid. With their big sombreros, casual dress and generally swashbuckling appearance, they look remarkably like the bandits they were meant to suppress! The officer (4) wears a campaign hat and has a pistol holster and short sword at his side, while the men (5) wear sombreros and carry slung rifles. All wear brown jackets and grey trousers. Produced 1913-40 and uncommon.

6-7 The Mexican infantry are sometimes found in a good second-grade type painting: the officer (6) in green and the men in blue (7) or red jackets.

8-10 Montenegrin Infantry; set 174.

From the rarest of the "Balkan Wars" sets, these figures are based on the Russian infantry shown at (1-2) *page 76*, but in grey with a red pill-box cap. The officer (8) is distinguished by a gold collar and cuffs and an extended sword arm, while the men carry rifles both at the trail and at the slope. An unusual variation uses the Dublin Fusiliers casting — see (23) *page 55* — with the pill-box cap.

11 Netherlands Infantry; set 1850. This infantryman uses the same casting as (12-13) and the Argentine infantry shown at (5-6) *page 66*, which are in turn derived from the German infantry figure. This very rare set in grey-green, which included an officer, was only available in 1939-40.

12-13 Polish Infantry; set 1856. This rare set was introduced in 1939, and available post-war from 1946-49. The infantryman (12) has the improved-pattern rifle introduced *c*1949. Dark blue-grey was an odd colour for the Poles, as in reality they wore khaki.

14 Serbian Infantry; set 173. Produced at the time of the Balkan Wars, this set of eight figures without an officer uses the charging Japanese figure (1) with a pill-box cap. The date on the base 16.1.1904 refers to the original Japanese rather than the Serbians, which were available from 1911 to the mid 1930s.

15 Spanish Cavalry, Review Order, with Officers; set 218. Produced in 1925, this splendid cavalryman uses a modified Scots Grey

5 **6** **7** **8** **9** **10**

16 **17** **18** **19** **20**

24 **25** **26** **27**

walking horse. Apart from the kepi which should be blue, the uniform is a good representation of a pre-1910 Hussar de Pavia. It was not issued post-war, and is rare.

16 Spanish Infantry; set 92. This rare set was issued in 1898 at the time of the Spanish-American war. This early version uses the valise equipment body — see (4-5) *page 50* — and has the correct type of Spanish shako known as a ''ros'', here with a white cover painted on. He carries a rifle at the trail, but in the left hand! The green facings indicate a rifle regiment.

17 Spanish Infantry; set 92, later version. This is a specially designed figure, and is equipped with a grey ''ros'' with plume and moulded ''wings'' on the point of the shoulder, with red line infantry

facings. The rifle is carried in the Spanish manner. This version of the set did not include an officer, and was discontinued in 1940.

18-19 Officer and man of the Svea Life Guard; set 2035. Instead of producing a new figure to represent the Swedish Life Guards, Britains re-used the pre-war Argentine cadet. The plumed helmet was correct, but the Swedes did not have frogging on their tunics. Britains therefore used the old toy soldier makers' maxim — if you don't paint it in, it isn't there! The officer (18) uses the same casting as the man (19), but with a sheathed sword in the left hand. The set was produced from 1949-59, and in 1966 as a seven-piece set, no. 9175.

20 Turkish Infantry: set 167. This

eight-piece set of Turkish infantry on guard in review order, without an officer, was introduced in 1911. Using the 1910 ''Buffs'' casting — see (21) *page 51* — but with a fez, they retained the gaiters right through to 1940.

21-22 Turkish Cavalry; set 71. This set was produced earlier than the Turkish infantry, in 1897. On early box labels the cavalry is specified as the ''Ertoghrul Regiment'' — see (1) *page 94*. The officer with extended sword arm (22), and the troopers with lances (21), all used the Indian Army cavalry figure shown at (1) *page 58*, with a fez. The set was available until 1940.

23-24 Uruguayan Cavalry; set 220. These handsome figures use the same casting as the Argentine cavalry — see (8-9) *page 67* —

but they have dark blue uniforms with red trouser stripes, and the men (24) have red lance pennants. The set was produced from 1925-40 and 1953-59.

25 Uruguayan Military School Cadet; set 221. A rare, very attractive and unique figure in a finely detailed Napoleonic-style uniform with a tall shako, from a set of eight without an officer produced from 1925-40 and 1948-52.

26-27 Uruguayan Military School Cadets, Marching at the Slope with Officer; set 2051. Strangely, Britains dropped their excellent earlier cadet figure in favour of one based on the standard infantry body, with a small kepi topped by a large plume. The result was still quite attractive, but it only lasted from 1953-59.

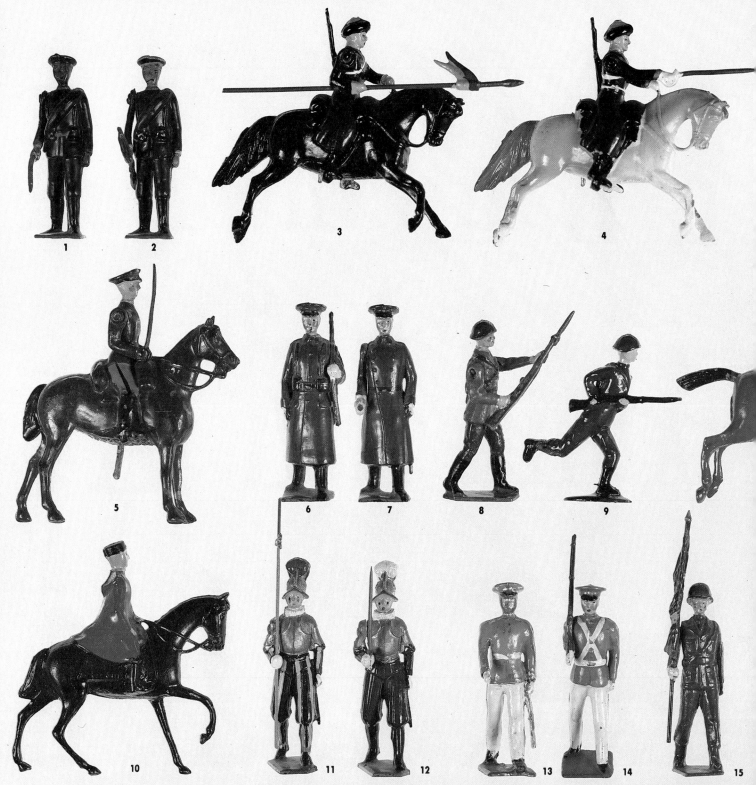

1-2 Russian Infantry; set 133. These Imperial Russian infantry were introduced in 1904 at the time of the Russo-Japanese War, and were available until 1940. The officer (1) has an extended sword arm; early sets had infantrymen both at the trail and at the slope. The infantryman (2) is from a later set that had men at the trail only.

3-4 Russian Cavalry (Cossacks); set 136. The officer (4) with his extended sword arm and the Cossack with lance both use the same casting, with their slung rifles cast integrally. Produced from 1904-40, and 1955-66.

5 Red Army, Cavalry Parade Uniform; set 2028. This figure is based on the French Foreign Legion officer — see (22) *page 70* — with a peaked cap. The officer

was on a grey and had an extended sword arm. The set was produced from 1949-59.

6-7 Red Army Guards Infantry, Parade Uniform, Greatcoats; set 2027. These figures were based on the Grenadier Guards in greatcoats — see (11-12) *page 48* — but with peaked caps and slung rifles. The officer (7) has an extended sword arm (the blade is missing). This set was available from 1949-59, and for the final year, 1966, as set 9172.

8 Red Army Infantry, Summer Uniform, Marching in Review; set 2032. Available from 1949-59, this Russian infantryman has a pair of movable arms and rifle moulded as one piece.

9 Red Army Infantry; set 152P. This New Crown range figure is based

on the charging Japanese — see (1) *page 74* — but with trousers modified into breeches, and the steel helmet head from (8).

10 Red Army Cossack; set 151P. Also from the New Crown range, this Cossack has probably been carefully repainted red, as this unusual figure should be in dark olive green like (9).

11-12 Papal Swiss Guards, with Officer; set 2022. These attractive figures, available from 1955-66, depict the Swiss Guards of the Vatican in their Renaissance-style uniforms. Using the same casting, the officer (12) has a sword at the carry, while the men carry halberds. The set contained nine pieces, later increased to 11.

13-14 Venezuelan Military School Cadets. In 1955 Britains produced

no less than five sets of the Venezuelan armed forces. The cadets (shown here in re-touched condition) are based on the US Marine Corps castings — see (1-2) *page 80* — but in light blue tunics and caps, white trousers and cross-belts. Set 2098 and 2099 contained seven and 15 cadets respectively, and were available until 1964. Set 2100, available until 1964, contained seven cadets and a plain-armed officer, as well as Venezuelan infantry and sailors.

15 Venezuelan Infantry, Service Dress. These were just the US infantry figures from set 2033 — see (29-30) *page 79* — in perhaps a lighter shade of olive drab, but the colour bearer shown is readily indentifiable by his flag in the red,

16 17 18 19 20 21 22 23
24 25 26 27
28 29 30 31

yellow and blue of Venezuela. They were available in set 2100, mentioned above, and in sets 2104 and 2105 from 1955-59.

16 Royal Canadian Mounted Police, Dismounted, in Winter Dress; set 214. Britains first depiction of the "Mounties" was a rugged figure in a stocking cap and short double-breasted coat. Introduced in 1925, he was available post-war only in a Picture Pack, no. 52B, with a greenish coat and without a bayonet.

17-18 Royal Canadian Mounted Police, Summer Dress, Marching; set 1554. Like the New Zealand infantry — see (26) *page 57* — this was introduced in 1937; it uses the same casting, but is empty-handed. The early small-headed version (17) was soon

replaced by a large-headed type (18). The set lasted until 1966.

19-21 Fort Henry Guards, with Mascot; set 2148. Fort Henry is a preserved fortress in Canada with a "re-enactment" unit, formed of students, who wear the British Army uniform of the 1860s. Produced from 1957-66, with a view to sales at Fort Henry, this set contained an officer (19) goat mascot (20) and five men (21).

22 Fort Henry Guards Pioneer; set 2182. The last completely new lead figure to be issued by Britains. The axe and two arms are a separate movable unit, which clips in at the shoulders. It was sold singly at Fort Henry from 1959-66.

23 Fort Henry Guards, 1812 War, 49th Foot; set 9155. This figure

with green facings is based on a Waterloo infantryman first issued in 1937. The same figure with black facings represents the 89th Foot from set 9160. Both were sold at Fort Henry in the 1960s.

24-25 Royal Canadian Mounted Police, Regulation Summer Dress, with Officer; set 1349. This set was first produced in 1934. The officer (25) is empty-handed, while the men (24) carry rifles. Available right through to 1966.

26 Mounted Officer of the Royal Canadian Mounted Police. This attractive figure first appeared boxed singly as no. 2066 in 1952, and replaced two of the men in set 1544 (18) the following year.

27 Royal Canadian Mounted Police at Attention. This scarce figure was only available as Picture

Pack 1267B from 1954-59 and in the "half-set" no. 2134 with (18) and (26) from 1957-59. It is based on the artillery man at attention — see (5) *page 86* — but with a "Mountie" head.

28-29 Canadian Governor General's Horse Guards; set 1631. The officer (29) is mounted on the rearing Household Cavalry officer's horse, and the men ride trotting horses and hold swords at the carry. They were available from 1938-40 and 1946-66.

30-31 Princess Patricia's Canadian Light Infantry; set 1633. These figures use the standard marching infantry castings, but with broad Wolseley helmets, and have light blue facings. They were produced from 1938-40 and after World War II from 1946-66.

1-4 United States Infantry; set
91.The first figures depicting US
infantry were introduced, along
with set 92: Spanish Infantry —
see (16) *page 75* — in 1898
during the Spanish-American
War. The figures use the valise
equipment casting with a
campaign hat (1). The first fixed-
arm, bemedalled officer was soon
replaced by this version (2) with a
movable sword arm. In 1906 a
new fixed-arm figure at the
shoulder arms, using the same
casting as the Boer — see (9)
page 55 — was introduced.
Shortly after this a third type
appeared, on guard with fixed
bayonet (3), with an officer using
the CIV casting (4); they remained
in production until 1940.
5 This interesting US cavalryman

at the gallop, using the same
casting as the fixed-arm Boer
cavalryman — see (15) *page 55*
— is probably a special painting.
See also (16).
6-12 American Soldiers; set 149.
These rare figures are from a
"Military Display and Game" set,
introduced in 1907 at the same
time as set 148: The Royal
Lancaster Regiment, which used
the same castings but with
foreign service helmets. The
game consisted of a card tray
with hinged metal clips attached,
into which the bases of the
soldiers could slide — this
feature necessitating the change
from oval to rectangular bases.
The figures having all been shot
down by matchstick gun, or
worse, (helping to account for

their rarity today!) they could be
brought back to life by flipping
them back upright. The figures in
the set, based on castings
already available, but with small-
crowned peaked caps, were as
follows: one mounted officer (6),
two gunners (7) with the gun from
the B-size artillery — (19) *page 47*
— one officer (12), one colour
bearer (8), one bugler (11), three
men running at the slope (9) and
three at the trail (10). The set was
available until about 1922.
13-14 US Infantry, Service Dress; set
227. This set, issued in 1925-40
and 1946-48, captures the look of
the World War I "doughboy"
rather well (14). The fixed-arm
officer (13) wears a peaked cap.
15,17 United States Cavalry, Service
Dress, Mounted at the Walk; set

229. This set used the new
casting, of a figure in a patch-
pocket tunic on a walking "Scots
Grey" type cavalry horse. (15)
shows the early light brown-khaki
finish, while (17) is a late example
in a grey-green uniform. The
cavalrymen were available in set
229 in 1925-40 and 1946-59, and
as Picture Pack 31B in 1954-59.
16 US Cavalry, Service Dress,
Galloping; set 276. Introduced in
1928, this figure uses the same
casting as the South African
mounted infantryman shown at (6)
page 56, which replaced the
former fixed-arm type at this time.
It was produced until 1940, and
as Picture Pack 39B in 1954-59.
18 USA Air Force Officers in Short
Coats; set 330. Introduced in
1929, this set contained eight

khaki officers as shown.

19 USA Air Force Officers in Flying Kit and Short Coats; set 332. This attractive figure was only produced as an American pilot, and never as an RAF figure.

20-21 United States Air Corps, 1949-pattern Blue Uniform; set 2044. Produced from 1950-65, this set used the same castings as the Australian infantry in blue dress — see (12-13) *page 56*. The men differ from the RAF figures at (41) *page 65* by having slung carbines and buff waist belts.

22 A post-war example of a second-grade US cavalryman, available from the 1930s onwards either boxed or for retail singly.

23-24 Second-grade US infantry. Note that the officer (23) is the same as (13) but in a simplified

paint finish, while the infantryman (24) is a fixed-arm figure.

25-26 Second-grade US infantry, standing and lying firing. There was also a kneeling firing figure. The standing figure (25) is based on the Gloucestershire Regiment casting — see (20) *page 55* — with a campaign hat, but the kneeling and lying figures with puttees are unique.

27 A Second-grade US infantryman "at the ready". Unlike (25-26) the figure is based on the gaitered British line infantry casting.

28 United States Military Police; set 2021. Oddly, when Britains brought out an up-to-date American soldier after the war it was specifically a "snowdrop", as the MPs were known, complete with cast-in armband

and holster, rather than an infantryman. Available from 1948-65, the set was reduced to seven pieces in 1960.

29-30 United States Infantry, Service Dress with Steel Helmets; set 2033 Replacing the "doughboys" of set 227, this set used the same rather slim casting as the Military Policeman. Because of this all ranks have superfluous armbands and cross-belts, and the men have pistol holsters, although these items are not painted in. Produced from 1949-66, the set was reduced to seven pieces in 1960.

31 Band of the United States Army in Khaki; set 2117. This bassoon player is from the new 12-piece band introduced in 1956, to replace the former peaked-cap United States Military Band, set

1301. New features included white steel helmets and plastic drums. Available until 1961.

32 United States Military Band in Full Dress Uniform; set 2110. A saxophonist from this colourful 25-piece band, produced from 1956-59 and then as set 9478 from 1961-63.

33 West Point Cadets, Winter Dress; set 226. These attractive and popular figures of the famous US military academy were available as a set of eight, without an officer, from 1925-40. Post-war they were included in set 232 from 1946-66.

34 West Point Cadets, Summer Dress; set 299. This is the same as set 226 (33), but with white trousers. Available from 1929-40, and 1946-66, and quite common.

1-2 United States Marines, Blue Uniform; set 228. A post-war officer and man from a set first introduced in 1925. In pre-war sets dark blue caps were worn and no officer was included, but one of the marines had red rank chevrons and trouser stripes to indicate a sergeant. Available from 1925-40 and 1946-66.

2-5 United States Marine Corps Colour Guard; set 2101. This was a four-figure set, as shown, with a special box illustrated at (10) *pages 94-95*. The escort (2 and 5) are just standard marine figures. The colour bearers are special castings, similar to the standard marine, but with the distinctive harness moulded on to the figures. The colours are cast metal, stencil painted, the USMC

flag red with the eagle, globe and anchor emblem.

6 A trumpeter from the Full Band of the United States Marine Corps, Summer Dress; set 2112. See *page 82* for the full set.

7 US Marine in Review Order; a second-grade figure, originally issued singly as no. 31C, but also available in a bewildering variety of ''A'' series sets and other categories at different times.

8 US Bluejacket; no. 92P in the New Crown range introduced in 1956. This late second-grade item is very similar overall to (9), but is a fixed-arm figure.

9 US Sailors (Bluejackets); set 230. This attractive set of eight US sailors in blue was available from 1925-40 but never included an officer. It is uncommon.

10-12 US Sailors (Whitejackets); set 1253. The sailors in white did not appear until 1933, but lasted right through until 1966. The first paint scheme included a blue collar and brown ammunition belt and gaiters (10), but soon after the post-war reappearance of this set the collar became white and the belt and gaiters a pale green (11). Originally a set of eight sailors only, an officer (12) was introduced from 1948, using the standard marching officer casting with a peaked cap, like the US Marine Corps officer at (1). The set was available from 1933-40 and 1946-66, and is more common than the bluejackets.

13 Union Cavalry Trooper at the halt, with Carbine; Picture Pack 1360B. This interesting

figure, which was not included in the ordinary Civil War cavalry sets, is based on the ''Continental'' horse at the halt — see (11) *page 70*. It was available from 1954-59.

14-15 Union Cavalry; set 2056. An officer and trooper from a set of five cavalry that also included a trumpeter. The officer, wearing a kepi and riding a grey horse, is based on the Indian cavalry figure shown at (1) *page 58*. The troopers (14) wear slouch hats, carry carbines and sit the ''Chasseurs à Cheval'' type horse — see (21) *page 70*. Made from 1951-66, the set was reduced to four pieces in 1960.

16-21 Union Infantry with Officer, Standard and Bugler; set 2059. This seven-piece set used

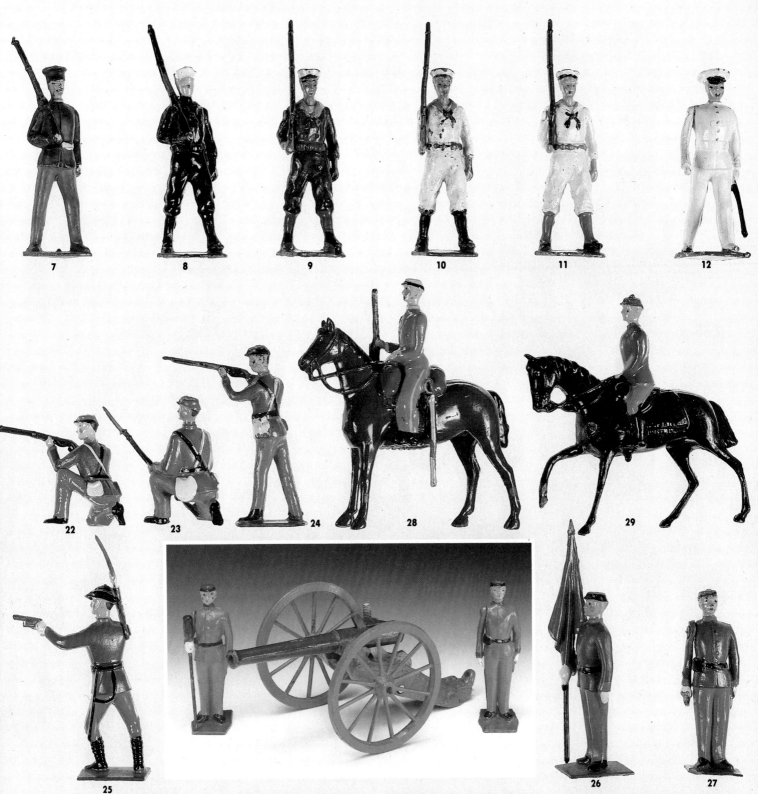

7   **8**   **9**   **10**   **11**   **12**

22   **23**   **24**   **28**   **29**

25   **26**   **27**

castings derived from the range of line infantry figures, with the officer based on that of the CIV. The standard bearer (16) is at attention with the ''Stars and Stripes'' at his side, the bugler (17) being the same figure with a straight bugle arm. The standing firing figure (18) uses the straight-trousered line infantryman casting. The set also included a kneeling firing man, as (22) but with a dark blue kepi and tunic; this was dropped in 1960. The figure standing at the ready (19) had gaiters, while the officer (20) can be distinguished from that in the early US infantry set — see (4) *page 78* — by the black hat and boots rather than brown. The set was completed by a figure kneeling to receive cavalry (21).

Available from 1951-66, the set was reduced to six figures in 1960; all the figures were also available as Picture Packs. An officer kneeling with binoculars was only available as a Picture Pack 1361B. A rare figure produced from 1954-56 was Picture Pack 1362B: Union Zouave charging; this was basically a late version of (4) *page 70*, with gold trouser stripes and a black top to his head-dress.

22-27 Confederate Infantry with Officer, Standard and Bugler; set 2060. Basically this seven-piece set used the same figures as the Union infantry, but with grey tunics and light blue tops to the kepis. One difference was that the Confederate infantryman at the ready (not shown), had a grey

Inset(above): *Confederate Artillery; set 2058. This, and the Union artillery set 2057, saw the reappearance of the pre-1930 field gun — see (7)page 47. These sets were available from 1951-66. The two Confederate gunners, correctly, have red facings, trouser stripes and kepi tops. The two Union artillerymen used the same castings but were dressed as (16-17) with the addition of red trouser stripes.*

slouch hat, brown ''butter nut'' tunic and white ''socks''. The set was produced from 1951-66, the Confederate kneeling to receive cavalry (21) being dropped when it was reduced to six pieces in 1960. All the Confederate infantry figures were issued individually in

Picture Packs, as was a kneeling officer with binoculars.

28 Confederate Cavalry Trooper at the Halt, with Carbine; Picture Pack 1365B. This was the equivalent of the Union cavalryman at the halt (13), but in a kepi. Also issued in Picture Packs, and using the same casting, were an officer with an extended sword arm on a grey horse, and a trumpeter. This was the only way to obtain a trumpeter; the Confederate cavalry set 2055 did not include one, containing only an officer similar to (15) and four troopers like (14) but with kepis.

29 An unusual second-grade Confederate cavalryman, available in some of the Crown range sets produced in the 1950s.

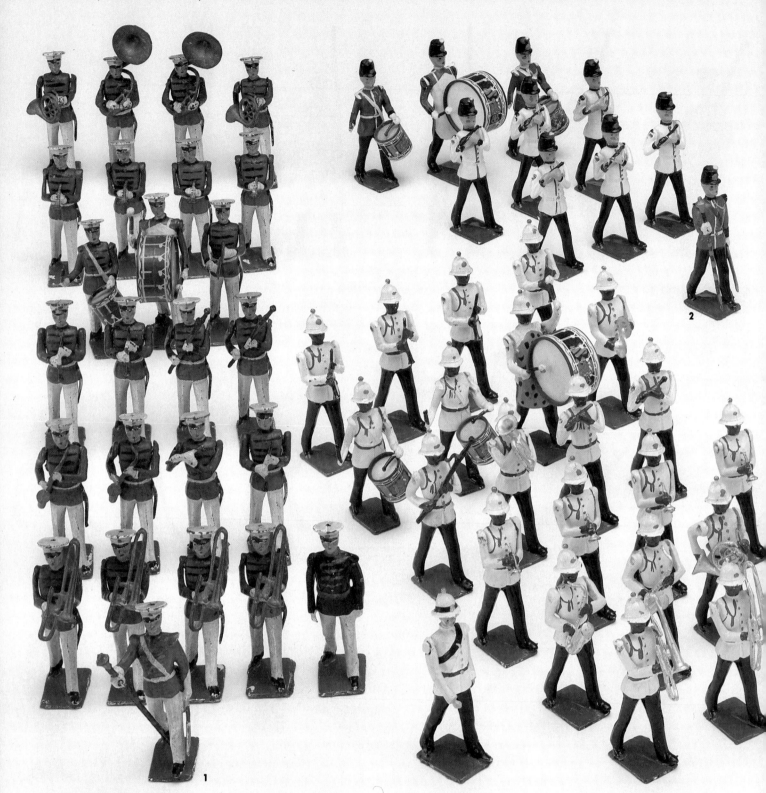

1 Full Band of the United States Marine Corps, Summer Dress; set 2112. This magnificent 25-piece band was only available from 1956-60, making it both rare and sought-after. While the rest of the Marine Corps had dark blue tunics in full dress, the band traditionally wore red with black frogging, and in summer dress — as depicted by this band — white trousers. The exception was the band leader, who wore a dark blue tunic with gold frogging. Britains based him on their adult bugler figure, but empty-handed. The drum major is based on the standard type, with peaked cap, red tunic with gold frogging, and staff. The musicians are playing,from the front: four trombones, two saxophones, one

fife, three clarinets, two bassoons, a side drum and bass drum in plastic, cymbals, four trumpets, two French horns and two sousaphones. This set replaced an earlier USMC band in review order: set 2014, available from 1948-55. This 21-piece band featured men in blue trousers, and metal drums.

2 Fort Henry Guards Band; set 2178. In 1959 two Fort Henry bands were introduced; they were really fife and drum corps. Set 2177 contained only five pieces — a drum major, bass drummer, side drummer and two fife players. This set was not listed in the main catalogue, but appears to have been sold at Fort Henry until 1966. Set 2178, illustrated, contains 10 pieces, and was only

produced very briefly. The drum major is based on the standard casting carrying a long mace, but with the black, slightly conical shako with a red and white pom-pom worn by all the Fort Henry guard figures. The six fife players are based on the usual musicians, with the short bandsman's sword, but wear white tunics as worn by British Army bands up to 1873. The boy side drummers and bass drummer have plastic drums.

3 Highland Pipe Band of the Black Watch; set 2109. This magnificent and colourful 20-piece band was introduced in 1956 and remained on sale until a year before lead soldier production ceased. It was based around 12 of the Black Watch pipers already available in set 11 — see (34) *page 53* — but

also introduced several new figures. The drum major is similar in style to the Highland officer on foot — see (22) *page 53* — but has a fixed right arm holding a mace, and the plaid billows out from the body. The pipers have black feather bonnets, a feature which they share only with the Scots Guards (all the other pipers wear glengarries). Whereas the rest of the band wear dark green Black Watch kilts the pipers have kilts and plaids in the bright Royal Stuart tartan. The bass drummer is a fixed-arm figure with his right arm raised above his head; he wears a tiger skin for an apron. The two tenor drummers also have tiger skin aprons; they have outstretched fixed arms and carry plastic drums of larger diameter

3

4

5

than those of the side drummers.
The side drummers are of adult
size, with movable left arms, and
have yellow aiguillettes across
their chests. This is an example of
a set produced relatively recently
and over a 10-year period, yet
highly valued by collectors.
4 Bahamas Police Band; set 2186.
The last band produced by
Britains, this is very rare indeed,
although not strictly military! With
a composition of 26 pieces it was
also the largest, but would appear
to have been for export only, not
being sold in the United Kingdom.
The bandsmen were based on the
Royal Marine castings — see (3)
pages 36-37 — but have white
tunics and dark brown skins, and
silver instruments rather than
brass. The bandmaster has a

European complexion, and is
based on the adult bugler figure,
but empty-handed, with a painted-
on black pouch belt and a band
round his helmet. The drum major
has a red sash and medals, and
the musicians have red
aiguillettes. The bass drummer
has a leopardskin apron, and both
he and the two side drummers
have plastic drums. The
percussion line is completed by a
cymbalist. As displayed here the
rest of the instruments are: front
rank — four trombones; second
rank — two saxophones and two
French horns; third rank — four
trumpets; fourth rank — one
bassoon, one euphonium and two
fifes; rear rank — four clarinets.
This set was produced only in
1959. There was also a smaller

version of the band in set 2185.
5 Band of the Royal Berkshire
Regiment; set 2093. Produced at
the same time as a series of
figures in 1953 Coronation Dress
— see *page 90* — this was
Britains' only band in the blue No.
1 Dress. The usual band figures
were used, in dark blue with red
bands around their peaked caps
to denote a Royal regiment. The
bandmaster is the usual officer
casting, marching empty-handed.
The drum major has a gold
baldrick, or cross belt, and a red
waist belt like the rest of the band.
The top of his mace is missing in
this example. This band has an
interesting selection of brass
instruments. The composition is:
front rank — two tenor horns and
two trombones; second and third

ranks — six clarinets, one fife
and one bassoon; fourth rank —
four trumpets; fifth rank — one
fixed-arm boy side drummer and
one bass drummer, both with
metal drums, and a cymbalist.
Plastic drums were introduced in
1956. The rear rank has, from the
left, two euphoniums, a bass tuba
and a double bass tuba. Sadly this
fine 25-piece band was produced
only from 1954-59, making it hard
to find. The keen collector should
note that there are two main
versions of this band — one with
metal drums, and the later
version from 1956 with plastic
drums and a boy fife player
instead of an adult one. All
Britains bands are collectable,
and those illustrated here are
particularly sought-after.

British Troops in Khaki by Britains, UK

1 Territorial Infantry; set 160. Introduced in 1980, this set had six peaked-cap infantrymen at the trail based on the Dublin Fusiliers figure — see (23) *page 55* — and a mounted officer like (17) but on a dark brown horse. With the outbreak of World War I the title soon changed to the British Expeditionary Force.

2-3 British Expeditionary Force; set 160. During World War I the contents of set 160 changed to these more accurate figures — a fixed-arm officer (2) and seven men (3) in peaked caps, service dress and 1908 webbing equipment. The name of this set reverted to Territorial Infantry in the early 1920s, and remained in the catalogue until 1940.

4-5 Infantry of the Line, Shrapnel-proof Helmets; set 195. These use the same casting as (3) but with a steel-helmet head; the officer carries a short ball-topped cane. Available from 1919-40, and post-war from 1946-59.

6 Royal Tank Corps; set 1250. This interesting figure also used the World War I infantry casting but with the Tank Corps' distinctive black beret. The set was produced from 1933-40.

7 The Devonshire Regiment; set 110. The early versions of the Dublin Fusiliers and Devonshires shown at (23-24) *page 55* could be distinguished by their different rifle positions. However, after World War I they were both depicted at the trail, using the new broader figure in 1908 webbing, the Dublin Fusiliers

being distinguished by sand-coloured trousers and helmets. The set was available until 1940 without an officer.

8-9 British Infantry, Tropical Service Dress; set 1294. These attractive figures, stepping off on the right foot, were available from 1934-40. The officer (8) uses the same casting as the man, but with a plain left arm.

10 Infantry in Steel Helmets and Gas Masks; set 258. A set of eight of these infantrymen, a modification of (3), without an officer, was produced from 1928-40.

11-15 A series of sets of "British Infantry in Steel Helmets and Gas Masks" was introduced in 1937. Set 1611 had seven prone figures and the flamboyant officer (15). Set 1612 had seven men throwing

grenades (13) and an officer (15). Both sets were available until 1940. Set 1613 was a seven-piece set of six charging figures (14) and an officer (15). It was available right through to 1966, latterly as a six-piece set. The unusual digging figure (11) was only available in Display Sets 1614 (until 1966) and 1615.

16-17 Yeomanry, Territorial Army; set 159. This set had five khaki cavalrymen in peaked caps, an officer with extended sword arm on a cantering grey horse (17) and four troopers with swords at the carry on trotting horses. It was produced from 1908-40.

18-19 21st Lancers; set 94. Originally issued in foreign service helmets — see (19) *page 55* — these figures were given steel helmets

84

10 11 12 13 14 15

22

19

21 23

24 25

20

34

35

36

37 38 39 40 41

during World War I. This quite uncommon set had a trumpeter on a grey horse (19) and four troopers holding lances with furled pennants, and was produced until 1940.

20 Machine-gun Section, Lying; set 194. This set contained six prone machine-gunners in peaked caps. Announced by Britains in 1916, it was available until 1940.

21 Machine-gun Section, Sitting; set 198. On its introduction in 1920 this set contained four seated machine-gunners and their guns, but was increased to six units in the 1930s. The set was produced until 1940.

22-23 Infantry with Peaked Caps, Standing, Kneeling and Lying Firing; set 1260. Introduced in 1933, the first figures had gaiters,

but these were soon changed to the full-trousered type. (22) shows a very unusual transitional form, a gaitered prone figure with splayed legs; the figure in gaiters usually has the legs together, while the full-trousered type has the legs splayed. (23) shows the later full-trousered kneeling figure.

24 British Infantry in Battledress, At Ease; set 1828. This unusual figure (actually in service dress) is based on the operator for the sound locator and predictor — see (17) *page 87* — but with the right arm holding a rifle in the "at ease" position and a plain left arm. The set is very rare.

25 The Home Guard Marching, with Slung Rifles; set 1918. This figure is in battledress without any equipment. The officer had a

plain left arm and a dark blue red-topped field service cap.

26-34 British Infantry (Steel Helmets) with Rifles and Tommy-guns, and Officer; set 1898. Most of the battledress soldiers shown here (26-34) were sold as second-grade figures, but set 1898, available in 1940 and post-war until 1963, contained four riflemen at the ready (26), an officer (27) and three tommy-gunners (31). Items (29) and (31) are particularly unusual; although hollow-cast battledress figures in identical poses were available, these two are solid mazak (zinc alloy) castings, probably produced in the 1950s to meet Australian toy safety regulations. (32-34) have large 1950s helmets.

35-36 Machine-gun Section (Lying

and Sitting); set 1318. This set combined a re-working of (21) — the seated machine-gunner now having an airborne forces-type rimless helmet and anklets — with the steel-helmeted version of the prone machine-gunner. The set was available until 1966.

37-38 British Infantry, wearing Full Battledress; set 1858. The officer (37) carries a baton in his right hand. The set was introduced in 1939; a Bren-gunner was added after the war, the set remaining available until 1959.

39-41 Airborne Infantry; set 2010. Introduced in 1948, this set was derived from the battledress infantry in set 1858 but with the Parachute Regiment's red beret. It included a man carrying a Bren gun and was available until 1960.

Vehicles, Artillery and Royal Engineers by Britains, UK

1-4 Royal Tank Corps. A squad of these figures were supplied with the Carden Loyd tank (22) in set 1322. See also (6) *page 84*.

5-6 Team of Royal Artillery Gunners, (Active Service); set 313. Introduced in 1929, this set contained four standing (5) and four kneeling (6) empty-handed figures in peaked caps.

7 An artillery officer in peaked cap with binoculars, derived from the line infantry figure.

8-9 Just before World War II the peaked-cap figures in set 313 received steel helmets.

10-13 Team of Gunners Carrying Shells; set 1730. Introduced in 1939, this set had three standing and four kneeling steel-helmeted figures carrying artillery shells. Post-war, the set contained an

officer with binoculars (19), two standing gunners (9) and two kneeling gunners (8) from set 313, one gunner standing with a shell (10) and two kneeling with shells (12). It was produced until 1962.

14 Sound Locator; no. 1638. This was a primitive pre-radar device for detecting the approach of enemy aircraft acoustically. Introduced in 1938 it was available briefly post-war.

15 Rangefinder, with Operator; no. 1639. This is mounted on wire tripod legs with a fixed-arm operator leaning forward to look through it. Available from 1938-40 and post-war until 1959.

16 Spotting Chair, Swivelling, with Man; no. 1731. The reclining observer has a movable left arm holding binoculars. Available from

1939-40 and 1946-59.

17-18 Predictor with Operator; no. 1728. A representation of an early form of mechanical computer for calculating the projected position of aircraft. Available from 1939-40 and 1946-59.

19 The later version artillery officer with binoculars in a steel helmet, from set 1730; see (10-13).

20 Height-Finder with Operator; no. 1729. This is similar in concept to the rangefinder, but larger. The operator is the same as (15) but shown here in the post-war paint finish. This item was available from 1939-40 and 1946-59.

21 Motor Machine-gun Corps; set 199. Introduced in the early 1920s, this set contained three of these units. The motorcycle and rider was a one-piece fixed-wheel

casting, four of which were available in set 200: Motorcycle Despatch Riders.

22 Tank of the Royal Tank Corps (Carden Loyd); set 1203. This was really a lightly-armoured machine-gun carrier, but it was designated a tank at a time of financial stringency. The first version, produced in 1933 had white rubber tracks. The later version, illustrated, was introduced in 1940 and has solid cast tracks with small wheels underneath.

23 Bren Gun Carrier and Crew; no. 1876, introduced in 1940 and available after the war until 1960.

24 Motorcycle Despatch Riders; set 1791. This four-piece set was introduced in 1939, replacing the fixed-wheel World War I motorcycles of set 200 (21) with a

Inset (above): *Royal Engineers vehicles. Set 203: Pontoon Section with Pontoon, Review Order, available 1922-39, comprised an open-framework wagon carrying a wooden pontoon boat and two sections of decking to form a bridge. Set 1330: Wagon, General Service Royal Engineers, in Review Order, was in effect two limbers or two-wheeled carts. Produced from 1934-40 and 1948-59, this is a late version.*

more up-to-date revolving wheel type. The rider wears a Royal Signals blue and white armband. The set was produced post-war until 1966, but from 1960 a peaked-cap battledress officer like (10) *page 56* replaced one of the motorcycles.

25 Staff Car with General and Driver; set 1448. First produced in 1936, this is an extensively modified version introduced in the early 1950s, which remained available until 1959.

26 Gun of the Royal Artillery; no. 1292. First introduced in 1934, this gun was available until 1967.

27 Gun of the Royal Artillery; no. 1263. This small, basic gun was produced from 1933 to 1967.

28 4.5in Howitzer; no. 1725. This is a rubber-tyred gun introduced in

1939 and available until 1967.

29 18in Heavy Howitzer on Tractor Wheels; no. 1265. This splendid piece had a very realistic breech-loading mechanism and ammunition incorporating spring-loaded shell-cases of different strengths to vary the range. Introduced in about 1920, it was available right up to 1980 in modified form.

30 18in Howitzer, Mounted for Garrison Duty; no. 1266. This is the same as (29) but on a static mounting.

31 Two-pounder Light AA Gun, Mobile Unit; no. 1717. This is the AA gun no. 1715, mounted on a four-wheel trailer with swing-out booms, available from 1939-40 and 1946-62.

32 Armoured Car with Swivelling

Gun; no. 1321. Introduced in 1934 and based on a Crossley armoured car, this is an early example with solid metal wheels.

33 Underslung Heavy-duty Lorry with Driver and Anti-aircraft Gun; no. 1643. This splendid 27cm (10.5in) long vehicle was available by itself or with loads such as this 4.5in AA gun. The gun, available separately as no. 1522, is one of the rarest of Britains weapons, produced from 1937-40. The underslung lorry was produced from 1938-40 and, with a round-nosed bonnet, briefly post-war.

34 Regulation Limber; no. 1726. This rubber-tyred limber with opening lid matched the 4.5in howitzer (28); introduced at the same time, it was available until 1960.

35 Mobile Searchlight; no. 1718.

This working searchlight was available separately, or on a trailer. Available from 1939-40 and from 1946-62.

36 Covered Army Tender, Caterpillar Type; no. 1433. The last of three versions of the half-track tender, produced from 1957-70.

1-2 Knights, Mounted and on Foot, 16th Century; set 1307. When introduced in 1934 set 1307 had two mounted and five foot knights, while set 1308 had five mounted and six foot figures. Post-war set 1308 was dropped, but set 1307 was enlarged to three mounted and six foot knights. When renumbered as set 9398, two more mounted knights were added, making an 11-piece set with the same composition as the original set 1308; this lasted right up to 1966. These are post-war examples, lacking the cast lance tips of pre-war versions.

3-8 Knights in Armour, with Squires, Herald and Marshal; set 1258. Introduced in 1933, the year before the 16th-century knights (1-2) these are by far the more

colourful figures. The two knights at (5) and (7) ride armoured mounts similar to (2) but these horses are strutting with their heads up. One knight (5) has a golden dragon device on his helmet and a red surcoat, lance pennant and horse trappings; the other (7) has a black plume, a surcoat and pennant in gold striped with red, and a blue saddle cover. The bearded marshal (4) sits a powerful-looking horse at the halt and carries his staff of office in a movable right arm. The squires at (3) and (8) carry long staffs with red and gold banners in their right hands. Their tunics and hose are quartered in black and brown, and each has a heraldic device on his chest surmounted by a deep collar or

cope in white. The herald's entire costume and trumpet banner (6) are quartered as though with the royal arms in gold on red and blue. The set was produced from 1933-40 and 1953-65.

9-13 Knights of Agincourt. In 1951 Roy Selwyn Smith produced this magnificent range of knights, for sale in the USA. The venture was not a financial success, but Britains recognized the excellence of these figures and bought the moulds, issuing them in 1954 as Knights of Agincourt. The mounted knights were boxed singly. An equally fine set of knights on foot, set 1664 (not shown) contained five figures in combat poses, two different men with lances and one each with sword, battle-axe and mace.

9 Knight with Sword; no. 1660. This figure has a gold-crested helmet and a blue-over-yellow shield, and holds his sword ready at his side.

10 Standard Bearer; no. 1662. The epitome of chivalry, this knight has his visor raised as he reins in his horse to a halt, holding aloft a standard charged with the Cross of St George.

11 Knight with Mace; no. 1659. This knight on a rearing horse brandishes a red-handled mace. His shield is divided horizontally blue over red to match the trappings of his horse.

12 Knight with Lance, Charging; no. 1661. He and his mount are clothed all in red except for a gold diagonal bar across his shield and the yellow reins on his horse.

13 Knight with Lance, Rearing; no.

1663. This knight has a closed visor and raised lance. The mounted knights were all available until 1966 — indeed the very last set of lead figures introduced by Britains, set 9392, contained the mounted standard bearer (10), four of the Agincourt knights on foot and four of the standing 16th-century knights (1); it was available from 1962-66.

14 Bedouin Arabs on Foot; set 187. This set was produced quite early by Britains, in 1913, long before they produced the Foreign Legion to oppose them. The Arabs wear an assortment of red, yellow and blue robes, all with white wrap-around burnooses. They carry jezails in their movable left arms. An eight-piece set, it was reduced to seven in 1960, its final year.

15 Bedouin Arabs, Mounted; set 164. These were produced even earlier than the foot figures, in 1911. Three men in the set have scimitars as (15) and two carry jezails like (18). They have white robes, and head-dresses and flowing cloaks in blue, green or red. Produced right up to 1966, the set lost one figure in 1960.

16-17 Arabs of the Desert, Mounted and on Foot; set 2046. This set, produced in 1950, introduced four running Arab figures (17), which had jezails, scimitars and spears and came in blue, red or green. The four horsemen included two with spears (16) which were only available in this set. Four walking Arabs (14) completed the set, which was produced until 1966.

18 Arabs of the Desert on Camels;

set 193. Six of these imposing pieces made up the set from 1919-40. The Bedouin and his camel were cast in one piece except for a movable arm holding a jezail. Two Arabs on camels were also included in set 224, with mounted and marching Arabs and some palm trees, this being the only way to acquire this splendid figure post-war.

19 Togoland Warriors with Bows and Arrows; set 202. This set contained eight of these figures in green, red and blue loin-cloths. The drawn bow and right arm are a separate casting. The set was produced from 1922-59.

20-22 Zulus of Africa; set 147. This set of eight appeared as early as 1906, the first version having oval bases. One basic slim figure is

used wearing assorted coloured loin-cloths, and running with a shield and two short spears in the left hand. The three different movable arms are: a spear in the throwing or stabbing position (20), a spear being carried or thrusting upwards (21) and a knobkerry or club (22). Set 147 was available until 1959, and a seven-piece set of Zulus, no. 9190, made an appearance in the final year of 1966. Set 188, available up to 1940, contained seven Zulus, two kraals (Zulu huts) and two palm trees with a scenic background.

23 This well-muscled Zulu, available in assorted coloured loin-cloths, with a rather fragile knobkerry which is often found broken, was a second-grade figure sold in both "A" series sets and singly.

1   2   3   4   5   6

7   8   9   10   11   12   13

14   15   16   17   18   19   20   2

1 Gentlemen-at-Arms with Officer; set 2149. This nine-piece set of the Sovereign's closest bodyguard was produced only from 1957-59 and is consequently rare. The officer carries a long black cane while the gentlemen have ornate halberds.

2 Her Majesty Queen Elizabeth II, Colonel-in-Chief of the Grenadier Guards; set 2065. The Queen in the uniform that she wears at the Trooping of the Colour ceremony. See also (8) *pages 94-95.* It was produced from 1952-66.

3-6 Yeoman of the Guard; sets 1257 and 1475. Set 1257 contained eight ''beefeaters'' in their Tudor-style costume, standing with their halberds held vertically (6), and an officer (3). Set 1475: Attendants to the State

Coach, contained footmen, dismounted outriders and four beefeaters which carried their halberds ''at the slope'' (4-5). The officer (3) is a slim figure in a plumed cocked hat and tailcoat, carrying a thin black staff. The first-version yeoman has his left hand on his hip (4), but this was changed to a straight left arm shortly before World War II (5-6). Set 1257 was available from 1933-62, and then as set 9300 with two extra yeoman until 1965.

7-9 The Royal Company of Archers, The Queen's Bodyguard for Scotland; set 2079. This interesting 13-piece set, depicting the ceremonial unit who act as the Sovereign's bodyguard when she is in Scotland, was introduced in 1953, Coronation year. The

officer was the same as (3) but in dark green with gold trim. The set contained four figures in each position: using their bows (7), standing with bows held upright (8) and standing with bows held parallel to the ground. It remained a 13-piece set until 1962 when as set 9302 it gained an extra figure (8), lasting until 1966.

10-11 5th Royal Inniskilling Dragoon Guards, Dismounted at Attention; set 2087. Both officer and man in this eight-piece set are based on the casting of the Guards officer at attention but with a peaked-cap head. The trooper (10) has silver chain-mail on the shoulders and a white waist belt, while the officer (11) has gold shoulder straps and a white-painted pouch belt.

12-13 Gloucestershire Regiment,

Marching at the Slope; set 2089. These figures wear the standard no. 1 dress for line infantry but with two distinctive features. The most obvious is the sky blue strip on the right arm representing the US Presidential Unit Citation awarded to the regiment for their conduct at the Imjin river during the Korean War, while the spot of gold at the back of the cap is the ''back badge'' commemorating the Battle of Alexandria of 1801, when the regiment, then the 28th Foot, repulsed simultaneous attacks in both front and rear.

14-15 Parachute Regiment Marching at the Slope; set 2092. These are basically the same castings as those of the Gloucestershires, but in the famous red berets.

16 Royal Irish Fusiliers at Attention;

set 2090. This interesting set used the Coldstream Guards at Attention castings, with the Irish Fusiliers' distinctive caubeen bonnets with green plumes.

17-18 Duke of Cornwall's Light Infantry, Marching at the Trail; set 2088. Based on the US Marine casting, these figures wear the Light Infantry no. 1 dress of dark green cap with lighter green band, dark green tunic, white waist belt and black trousers.

19 Rifle Brigade, Marching at the Trail; set 2091. These figures are similar to (18) but the uniform is dark green throughout with a black belt and gloves.

20-21 King's Royal Rifle Corps, Marching at the Trail; set 2072. Although not in no. 1 dress, these figures replaced the running Rifle

Corps in set 98 — see (33-35) *page 49* — as being more appropriate to a coronation procession. Available 1953-59.

22-24 Officers of the General Staff; set 201. This set consisted of a field marshal (24), a general (23) and two aide-de-camps (22) — one on a grey horse and one on a black horse. Britains seem to have been rather confused here. Only field marshals wore white breeches and over-the-knee "jacked" boots, while generals wore blue breeches and below-the-knee "butcher" boots. The casting for (23) actually represents a field marshal, while that for (24) portrays a general! On later examples Britains reversed the painting on these two figures. The set was produced from

1922-40 and also from 1946-59.

25 This fixed-arm general officer on a "sway-back" horse was available only in the large Display Sets 73, 131 and 132, from 1897-1922.

26-28 The "H" series consisted of just these three 70mm (2.75in) figures in second-grade painting: (26) no. 4H: Infantry of the Line; no. 5H: Foot Guard (although listed as such, he is in fact a fusilier); and (28) no. 6H: Highlander. They were available from the 1920s to the 1940s.

29-30 Waterloo Gunners; set 2152. In 1937, Britains produced Waterloo line infantry and Highlanders. The infantry were similar to (23) *page 77*, but with muskets at the shoulder arms. In 1957 these gunners were introduced. Based

on the same figure, but in blue jackets with red facings, they accompanied the gun illustrated in the *inset* on *page 81*. They were available until 1965.

31 Soldiers to Shoot; set 25. A battered example from a box of four, of an interesting novelty item — a slightly overscale line infantryman with a hollow-barrelled rifle that can fire a projectile by means of a strip of steel spring. It was produced from 1985 to the end of World War I.

32 Ski Trooper in White Snow Uniform; set 2037. This unusual piece was available individually boxed under this set number from 1949-59, and in the four-piece set 2017 from 1948-57. The rifle which originally clipped down the side of the pack is missing.

Small-scale Figures by Britains, UK

1

2

3

4

9

10

11

12

13

14

15

16

17

25

18

19

20

21

22

23

24

30

35

36

37

38   39

From 1896 until 1940 Britains produced a range of small-size figures, the infantry being about 44mm (1.73in) high and the cavalry 55mm (2.16in), known as the ''B'' and later the ''W'' series.

1 Trooper of the 1st Life Guards; set 1B. This is a late fixed-arm figure.
2 Trooper, 2nd Life Guards; set 7B. He has a movable carbine arm.
3 Horse Guards trooper; set 2B. His sword blade rests on his shoulder, and he rides a smaller horse than (2).
4 Horse Guards officer; set 2B. Basically the same figure as (3), but with an extended sword arm.
5 1st Dragoon Guards trooper; set 5B; with the early short carbine.
6 A later 1st Dragoon Guard on a larger ''walk-march'' horse.

7 This mystery figure has the black plume and blue facings of the 1st Royal Dragoons, although Britains did not list this regiment in their ''B'' series.
8 16th Lancers (Active Service) trooper; set 12B. Usually depicted in khaki — see (28-29) — this variant wears the 16th Lancers full dress scarlet tunic.
9 Grenadier Guards, Running, Slope Arms; set 18B. Note the ''daylight'' between the body and the slope rifle — compare (18).
10 Coldstream Guards, Marching at the Slope; set 16B. The same figures were produced as Scots Guards in Display Set 85.
11 Northumberland Fusiliers, Active Service Order; set 21B. An officer figure was produced by snipping away the rifle.

12 The Manchester Regiment, at the Slope; set 20B. A line infantryman in spiked helmet — see also (20).
13 Lancashire Fusiliers, Marching at the Trail; set 17B. The box for this set is shown at (7) *pages 94-95.*
14 Royal Dublin Fusiliers, Running at the Trail; set 19B. The ''B'' range was well endowed with fusilier regiments.
15 Cameron Highlander, in red doublet and white spiked helmet rather than the usual active service version (16).
16 The Queen's Own Cameron Highlanders, Active Service Order; set 23B. Strangely the figures in this set always seem to be painted with Black Watch kilts.
17 Bluejackets of the Royal Navy; set 22B. These sailors at the slope were also produced as

whitejackets in set 24B. See (24).
18 Grenadier Guards; 11W, later 161W. The slightly taller but simpler ''W'' version of Grenadier. Note that the numbering system of the ''W'' series changed in the 1930s from single and double figure numbers to a sequence starting at 145W.
19 Northumberland Fusiliers; set 21B. This is the later, taller square-based version of (11).
20 Infantry of the Line; 10W or 151W. This set was still sometimes labelled as the Manchester Regiment. Compare with (12).
21 Lancashire Fusiliers; 17B. A late version of the ''B'' series figure — compare with (13).
22 Running fusilier. Apparently an early ''W'' series figure, although fusiliers were deleted from this

92

range at a relatively early date.

23 Cameron Highlander, Full Dress; 23B. A late "B" series Highlander marching at the slope, with a feather bonnet. This casting was also in the "W" series.

24 Whitejackets of the Royal Navy; set 24B. This is the later version sailor — compare with (17).

25-26 Royal Scots Greys; set 6B. Two versions of the Scots Greys, on trotting (25) and galloping (26) horses — there were sometimes several different types of horse within a "B" series cavalry set.

27 An outrider from an RHA Active Service Gun Team; no. 126B. See (19-24) *pages 46-47.*

28 16th Lancers, Active Service Order; set 12B. The 16th Lancers trooper in the more usual all-khaki uniform — compare with (8).

29 16th Lancers, Active Service Order; set 12B. A late-version trooper on the large "walk-march" horse — see also (6).

30 11th Hussars; set 10B. An early trooper with short carbine.

31 11th Hussars; set 10B. A late-version trooper with a long carbine, on a large horse.

32 An outrider from the RHA Review Order Gun Team; set 125B. This used the same gun and limber as (19-24) *pages 46-47.*

33 Mounted Infantry; set 15B. An interesting figure in a scarlet tunic, khaki breeches and blue field service cap.

34 17th Lancers; set 13B. A trooper in full dress.

35 Egyptian Camel Corps; set 68N. Although compatible in size with the "W" range, this figure was

listed in the "N" range of second-grade standard-size figures.

36 Japanese Cavalry; set 11B. The only "foreign" troops in the original "B" series were Japanese and Russians — who were at war in 1904-5.

37 Russian Cavalry (Cossacks); 14B. Although based on the galloping horse, this is a unique figure. The tail is missing from this example.

38 Japanese Infantry; set 25B. This late-version Japanese soldier uses the Dublin Fusilier (14) with a head-change.

39 US Infantry (Service Dress); 55W, later 158W. A miniature version of the standard-size second-grade "doughboy" — see (24) *page 78.*

40 Russian Infantry; set 26B. Based on the running Grenadier Guard figure, Russian infantry are also

found marching at the trail.

41 French infantryman in greatcoat, from Britains' Paris Office.

42 A Belgian infantryman from the Paris Office. This is a different paint version of (41).

43 French infantryman in tunic, from the Paris Office. An officer was produced by snipping off the rifle.

44 French Infanterie Coloniale from the Paris Office. An ingenious re-use of (19) with the correct double row of buttons painted on.

45 A German infantryman, also from the Paris Office, and based on the later Manchester Regiment (20).

46-48 A cowboy and two North American Indians, included because they are quite rare "W" figures. (46) and (48) are miniature versions of figures in the "A" series.

The earliest Britains boxes and labels were quite simple with just the name of the set in bold type, some reference to it being best-quality English, British or London made, and the facsimile "W. Britain" signature. Set numbering did not start until about 1898, the number appearing initially on the box top label, and later on the end of the box lid with the set title. At first the soldiers nestled into paper and straw packing, sometimes with partitions between the figures. Later figures were slotted into diagonal slits in a card base, and from the 1930s tied to a backing card. Labels soon became more richly ornamented and were sometimes illustrated. From about 1906 Britains started to use the

services of Fred Whisstock, a freelance artist from Southend. Whisstock's box labels, which he signed, usually combined a regimental badge or insignia, battle honours and an illustration, sometimes rather naïve, of figures from the set. During World War I Whisstock was called up for military service, and on some labels produced at this time he rather quaintly prefixed his signature with "L/CPL" or "CPL" (lance corporal or corporal) — see (9). He went on designing for Britains until about 1928. In the 1930s more standardized labels started to appear, such as the "Types of the Colonial Army" shown at (5) and "Armies of the World". After World War II Britains used more general-purpose

"Regiments of all Nations" labels in colour on a buff background. In 1961, what was left of the lead soldier range was put into cellophane-fronted cartons. "Picture Packs" did not have cellophane windows, but were small boxes for single figures.

1 An interesting early label for set 71, the Turkish Cavalry introduced in 1897, specifically naming it as the Ertoghrul Regiment. For the figures in this set see (21-22) *page 74.* An article in the *Navy and Army Illustrated* for February 5th 1897, on the Imperial Ottoman Army, included a photograph of a detachment of the Ertogrul (*sic*) Regiment. The caption read in part "The Ertogrul Regiment is famous in the

service, and is a splendid corps. It is one of those which regularly mount guard upon the occasions of the Sultan's public appearances. Determination and warlike vigour seem to sit upon the faces of the men". The title of set 71 was soon changed to the "Turkish Cavalry".

2 The West India Regiment; set 19. An early illustrated label including battle honours, showing the regiment in action and in camp. See (23-24) *page 57* for figures from this set.

3 The Worcestershire Regiment; set 18. A late 1930s Whisstock box, with battle honours and the regimental badge on the label, but no illustration of the contents. The contents of this box — an officer, drummer, standing and kneeling

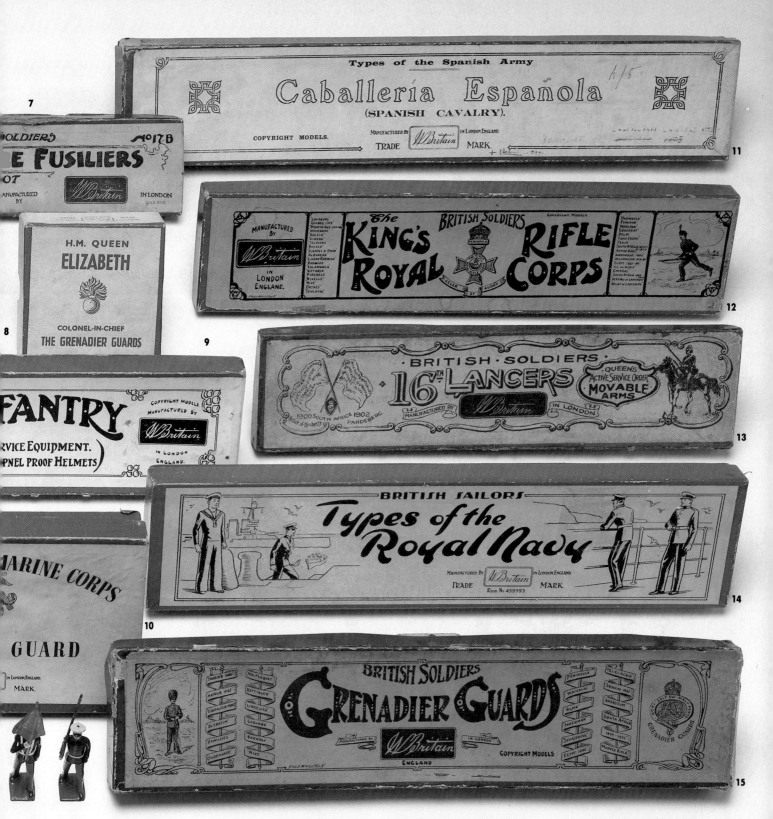

figures are shown — are very unusual. The Worcestershire Regiment are normally depicted in white helmets and white facings, but in 1937 Britains introduced a short-lived range of 47 sets covering virtually all the British infantry regiments, and in this series the Worcestershires were shown with blue helmets and green facings.

4 Machine Gun Section (Sitting Position); set 198. The small, 1920s box for this set in its early form when it contained four, rather than six, seated machine-gunners and their guns — see (21) *page 85*.

5 "Types of the Colonial Army", one of the standardized labels brought out in the mid-1930s.

6 5th Dragoon Guards; set 3. A late

1890s box designed to take small "Germanic" style cavalrymen; note that it is shorter than later cavalry boxes (1 and 11). For later-version 5th Dragoon Guards see (6-7) *page 40*.

7 The Lancashire Fusiliers; set 17B. A small box to take seven of the 44mm (1.73in) size "B" series infantry from about 1910 — see (13) *page 92*.

8 H.M. Queen Elizabeth, Colonel-in-Chief, The Grenadier Guards; no. 2065. The special individual box for the fine model of the Queen also shown at (2) *page 90*.

9 British Infantry, Shrapnel Proof Helmets; set 195. A set introduced during World War I. For the figures from this set see (4-5) *page 84*.

10 United States Marine Corps

Colour Guard; set 2101. The special box and label for the four-piece set shown here, and in another view at (2-5) *page 80*.

11 Spanish Cavalry; set 218. The elegant and simple label for a now rare and desirable set, only produced from 1925-40, shown at (15) *page 74*.

12 The King's Royal Rifle Corps; set 98. A Fred Whisstock label from c1910, with the Rifle Corps badge flanked by battle honours up to the South African War. See (33-35) *page 49* for Rifle Corps figures.

13 16th Lancers, Active Service Order; set 12B. A box to take four "B" size cavalry, c1910. The label is almost confusingly ornate, with battle honours on flags — those for South Africa added on below — while the rather good

illustration is squeezed into a corner. For examples of "B" series 16th Lancers see *page 93*.

14 "Types of the Royal Navy". Like (5), this is a "general purpose" label from the 1930s.

15 Grenadier Guards Firing; set 34. Although the Whisstock illustration on this label shows a Guardsman in the old "at ease" position this set contained a marching officer, drummer boy, and eight men firing. The battle honours are nicely portrayed, the Grenadier Guards crest incorporates the cipher of Edward VII (1901-10) and the label is bordered with flowing art nouveau tracery. This box dates from about 1910; earlier and later Grenadier Guards are shown at (1, 4 and 13-15) on *page 48*.

At the beginning of the century the British public in general were proud of the feats of arms achieved by the British forces in the many small colonial wars and campaigns fought throughout the 19th century. The use of artillery was often a decisive factor in these conflicts, and most British manufacturers were quick to realize that, as a major arm of the forces, the gunners needed to be reproduced in model form. Although variable in quality, these cannons and field guns were, from the earliest releases, often quite realistic in appearance and effective in operation.

All the larger British toy soldier manufacturers listed field pieces in their ranges. They were, when combined with figures or complete horse teams to draw them, usually among the most prestigious items in their catalogues as well as the most expensive. Lavishly boxed and presented they represented, then as now, a major acquisition for the keen collector.

Based usually on British Army units of the Royal Horse or Royal Field Artillery, and Royal Navy landing party crews, they appealed strongly to a public who had often seen the real-life counterparts in action — if only at the annual Royal Military Tournament in London.

Their obvious fragility, and the rough use often meted out to them — quite apart from the limited numbers in which, as expensive toys, they were sold — makes all gun teams among the rarest toy soldiers found today. Due to the variable quality of the models made by companies other than Britains, however, this is not always reflected in their value. The occasional foray into gun teams of countries other than the UK was usually accomplished by a simple repainting of an existing casting, or at most, the provision of an alternative head moulding. Some companies used a pre-existing cavalry horse as the basis for their artillery draught horses, in an attempt to reduce the high cost of moulds which would otherwise be relatively little used. One maker used a simple pin to transform a marching figure into one capable of holding a rope attached to a field gun.

The guns themselves were invariably capable of firing small shells, and indirectly added to manufacturers' sales by destroying figures which they were targeted on. Most makers also sold the guns separately, so they are in themselves less rare than complete teams.

1 Royal Navy field gun crew; by Reka, c1915. This small set was made up of the standard Reka field gun and three Royal Navy bluejackets marching. These were on a small wood and papier-mâché base incorporating a three-sided wall and earth banking. The only distinguishing features from the standard sailors are the gold trims on the hatbands and a small gold

insignia on the petty officer's right arm (rearmost figure). This is a rare set with the original box.

2 Royal Artillery, Territorials; Crescent catalogue no. 809, issued 1931-1950s. This galloping gun team was first made by Reka in 1921 and was one of the moulds sold to Crescent in 1930. The painting of the horses and figures is generally poorer than the Reka sets, which are now rare; they can also be identified by the erasing of the trade-mark below the horses in pre-World War II sets, and by the Crescent trade-mark from 1946. The gun is fired by a simple spring plunger mechanism, similar to French cannons, and the limber usually has a thin card or ply back and carries no ammunition. They are

both painted grey, with copper coloured wheels. The figures are of "standard" 54mm (2.12in) scale and were also issued as Royal Horse Artillery, in full dress, and steel-helmeted active service versions. The Reka originals were also made as USA and British Colonial sets.

3 Russian artillery officer; from the BMC series by Soldarma, c1921. This rare figure, normally part of the Royal Horse Artillery gun team shown at (4), is actually part of an identical set with green uniforms sold as Imperial Russian troops. The horse and rider are to 60mm (2.36in) scale.

4 Royal Horse Artillery, active service dress; from the BMC series by Soldarma, c1921. This well-sculpted and lively gun team

makes even the Britains issues look pedestrian and second-rate in comparison. It uses a gun and limber by Rivollet of France, with a spring mechanism as in the Reka set (2). It was also painted in Russian and USA uniforms on the same castings which are to 60mm (2.36in) scale. All are rare.

5 British Naval Brigade; by Reka, c1915. This set utilizes the original gun and limber for the set shown at (2). The far superior limber incorporates a lifting panel at the back to enable the 25mm (1in) long steel rod ammunition to be carried. The figures are the same as those shown at (1) but by inserting pins into the mould a "ring hand" was produced enabling them to pull a "draw rope" from the limber. Made to accompany a horse

team originally, the limber and gun were not issued with them until 1921 due to World War I. This set was also issued by Crescent after 1931 but with the figures reduced to six and without the limber. Crescent also used the original Reka artwork for their labels. Made to 54mm (2.12in) scale it is rare as either a Reka or Crescent set.

6 Fifteen-pounder field gun; by Renvoize, c1902. A patented design with a unique double-action firing mechanism, this was one of the most powerful "scale" guns made in Britain. It was sold singly and as part of a team which only differed from the Britains original in the movable arms of the riders and slight changes to the horses. It is a rare piece.

C.D. Abel, of Islington, London, c1898-1914, issued a large series of British Army regiments in various drill positions, and in 1902 patented a drill display frame on which their figures, re-issued with socketed base mouldings in special sets, could be paraded. A. Fry (The Erecto Toy Co. Ltd.) of Tottenham, London, c1915-22, concentrated on the Allied and Axis armies of World War I, and had perhaps the largest variety of action poses of any company. The Wellington Toy Company, of Liverpool, c1906-23, produced a range of simple, fixed-arm figures which were remarkable mostly for their cheapness.

1-3 Gordon Highlanders; by C.D. Abel, c1898. These rare Scots

figures, marching at the slope with fixed bayonets, were among the earliest issues by this company. They are to 54mm (2.12in) "standard" scale.
4-6 Royal Fusiliers; by Abel, c1902. These are the reissued version of Abel's basic marching figure, with the brass socket at the front of the base and locating blocks at the rear clearly visible. In sets of eight with no officer, and in a display drill set of 25 including a small mounted officer, they are slightly under "standard" scale.
7-9 Line infantry; by Abel, c1900. Although similar in appearance to (4-6) these rare figures are of earlier issue with sloped arms on the left shoulder. Slightly smaller than "standard" scale.
10 Line infantry; by Abel, c1902. This

Above: This typical Fry label, with its line drawing and mention of British labour and capital, was also used as a trade advertisement.

uses an improved base, as on (4-6), on an identical figure to (7-9) — but painted as a different British Regiment. It is slightly smaller than "standard" scale.

11 Line Infantry; by Abel, c1900. This figure was once attributed to Renvoize, but has now been identified by the identical head casting to (13) and the Abel slope

10   11   12   13   14   15

22   23   24   25   26

32   33   34   35   36   37   38

arm, as shown at (1-6). Small "standard" scale.

12 British line infantry officer; by Abel, c1902. A 40mm (1.57in) scale mounted figure.

13 Somerset Light Infantry; by Abel, c1900. This rare 54mm (2.12in) scale figure standing at attention has also been found with the simple holed base as at (9).

14 Scots Guard; by Abel, c1900. Also found painted as a Coldstream or Grenadier Guard, this rare 54mm (2.12in) figure may have been restricted to pre-1902 sets as the Guards are most commonly found on the (7-11) style figure.

15 British Camel Corps; by Abel, c1904. An intermediate 45mm (1.77in) scale figure, and a registered design, this is most

commonly found in gilt finish.

16 Royal Navy whitejacket, advancing with fixed bayonet; by Fry, c1915. "Standard" scale.

17 Royal Navy whitejacket, lying firing; by Fry, c1916. This is also found in the same variations as (16), but usually as a khaki "Tommy". "Standard" scale.

18 A post-1922 re-cast of the original Fry figure at (19), with poorer painting and no base trade-mark.

19 Italian Bersaglieri; by Fry, c1916. A smaller than "standard" figure.

20-21 London Scottish; by Fry, c1915. Two versions of this Territorial unit. "Standard" scale.

22 Gordon Highlander; by Fry, c1915. This rare figure is the same casting as (21).

23 Belgian infantry; by Fry, c1916. This larger than usual kneeling

figure is to 60mm (2.36in) scale.

24 French infantry; by Fry, c1916. A rare figure, slightly larger than "standard" 54mm (2.12in) scale.

25 New Zealander; by Fry, c1916. The silver-painted hat on this larger than "standard" figure is intended to represent the helmet issued to the Allies in 1916.

26 US "doughboy"; by Fry, c1918. A variation on (25) but using a new mould. Large "standard" scale.

27-28 Machine-gunners; by Fry, c1916. This painting of figures in khaki and full dress was a common way to add colour to the drab realism of the then "modern armies". 45mm (1.77in) scale.

29 Motorcycle despatch rider; by Fry, c1916. A small-size model of the Sunbeam motorcycle often used by despatch riders.

30 Red Cross nurse; by Fry, c1916. A fairly common "standard" scale figure, rarely found as a gilt-painted "Edith Cavell".

31 Austrian soldier by Fry; c1916. This rare figure is in the first movement of the "Order Arms".

32 Trench bomber; by Fry, c1916. Another steel-helmeted figure, to "standard" scale.

33 The Gentleman in Khaki; by Fry, c1916. An imaginative "standard" scale model of the famous Boer War illustration.

34-35 British officers; by WTC, c1916. The RAMC officer (34) has often been wrongly identified as a Fry figure. "Standard" scale.

36-38 Infantry marching at the slope; by WTC, c1916-23. Some of the many variations of these basic "standard" scale models.

1
2
5
6
8
3
4
7
12
13
14
15
16
17
18
19
27
28
29
30
31
32

The firms of Renvoize and Hanks Bros are regarded as the "Pirate Kings" of the early competitors of Britains. It is believed that Renvoize had many of its figures made in Germany, possibly by Heyde or Heinrich, as being primarily toy wholesalers they had suffered from Britains' inroads into the trade market. Hanks Bros were former Britains staff who set up in Hackney, London in 1900, issuing straight copies of early sets by Britains. The painting was inferior and the designs crude by comparison. All the figures shown are to "standard" 54mm (2.12in) scale.

1 Guardsman kneeling firing; by Renvoize, c1900. This figure uses the "blanket roll" body normally

employed for the Japanese and Russian versions.
2 Line infantry; by Renvoize, c1900. This is the usual body for (1) and is also found as a white-helmeted issue for "foreign service".
3 Japanese infantry; by Renvoize, probably post-1904. This casting was also used as a Russian with a green uniform.
4-7 British infantry, Boer War; by Renvoize, c1900. This selection of poses, some such as (5) and (6) closely resembling Britains, clearly show the incorrect facing colours — brown and black — typical of German-painted figures. This probably came about because of the incorrect reproduction of shades of colour on early black and white film, yellow appearing darker than red.

This was then misinterpreted on painting. The "foreign service helmet" was made by cutting off the line infantry helmet spike, but some such as (6) were missed. All are rare figures.
8 Line infantry officer; by Hanks, c1900. A copy of a Britains figure distinguishable by the light metal used and poor flesh colours.
9 Dragoon; by Hanks, c1900. A copy of a pre-1900 Britains casting, part painted in gilt. These were sold as seaside souvenirs.
10 Indian lancer, by Hanks, c1900. This rare figure can only be detected as a copy by the lance and large arm stub.
11 Lancer officer; by Hanks, c1900. This is another rare "pirate" which can be detected by the poor colour of the skin, the large

arm stub and the light metal.
12 Highlander; by Renvoize, c1900. A further example of incorrect painting, this is an original figure, very "Germanic" in style.
13 Gordon Highlander; by Renvoize, c1900. This rare figure is a more realistic finish of (12), which was sold in sets of ten with no officer.
14 Japanese infantry; by Renvoize, c1904. An alternative version of (6), closely resembling a Britains "volley" firing figure.
15 Guardsman; by Renvoize, c1900. A gilt figure, very close to the Britains original, this was possibly later issued by another firm.
16-17 Figures at attention. On the left is a Renvoize Guardsman of c1900, and the gilt figure is by an unknown manufacturer.
18 Russian 21st Line Regiment; by

9   10   11

20 21 22 23 24 25 26

33   34   35 36   37   38   39   40

Renvoize, c1904. This original figure is quite well sculpted; it was sold in sets of eight.

19 Royal Navy bluejacket; by Renvoize, c1900. This is another original. Marching figures by Renvoize do not seem to have been pirated, so they may date from after the 1900 prosecution by Britains for breach of copyright.

20 "Plug handed" Highlander; by Hanks, c1900. A fixed bayonet indicates that this copy is a Hanks pirate — not a Renvoize as is often thought.

21 Scots Guards piper; by Hanks, c1900. Again the painting and light weight identify this as a copy of a Britains figure.

22 Highlander, marching; a Hanks original, c1914. The offset diamond base is for fitting to a

shooting game patented in 1914.

23-24 Royal Navy officer and whitejacket; by Hanks, c1900. The fixed-bayonet sailor is a close copy of a Britains figure.

25-26 Zulus; by Hanks, c1912. These are nicely painted, animated originals of a favourite subject. (25) was, ironically, pirated by other makers after World War I.

27 Gordon Highlander piper; by Renvoize, c1900. This casting is also found as Scots Guards and Black Watch figures, but so rarely that they may have been issued only singly in sets with (28-29).

28-29 Highlanders marching; by Renvoize, c1904. These figures, rarely found with their frail arms intact, can be recognized by their similar stance to (19) and (30) and by their typical Renvoize-style

arms. Now rare, they were sold in sets of eight including a piper as shown at (27).

30 Irish Guard; by Renvoize, c1905. Repeating an error common to many makers, the bearskin plume is green and not St Patrick's blue.

31 Imperial Yeoman by Renvoize, c1900. The subject of a court action by Britains, these are very rare as they and their moulds were ordered to be destroyed.

32 Imperial Japanese cavalry; by Renvoize, c1904. This unusual movable-arm mounted figure still betrays its Britains-inspired origin, despite the gilt finish.

33 A kneeling gilt infantryman, produced by the same unknown maker as (17); a flaw in the casting shows it originated as the Hanks figure shown at (34).

34 Line infantry; by Hanks, c1900. This figure, although similar to Britains, is not a direct re-cast. It is rarely found intact.

35-37 Line infantry; by Hanks, c1900. Again, although the similarity to Britains figures is evident these are altered in pose and size sufficiently to avoid an accusation of direct re-casting. (37) has the typical Hanks rifle and bayonet.

38-40 Scots Guards officer, bugler and Guardsman, marching; by Hanks, c1900. These figures use the same basic body castings as (35-37) but with a different head and with a slope arms rifle instead of a rifle at the trail. This head interchangability marked a major step forward for most makers, enabling them to expand their ranges more economically.

An established toy wholesaler in London, Chas. W. Baker was, by 1900, already offering "toy soldiers made exclusively for us". By 1910 he had registered the trade-mark Reka, which was a simple reversal of part of his surname, and issued toy figures bearing that mark. He also used the phrase "British Make" instead of the more common "Made in Great Britain" on his figures and horses, so this can also be used for identification. Most of these figures are 54mm (2.12in) "standard" scale.

1 Coldstream Guard; c1900. To date this rare figure has only been found with this head, painted as several Guards regiments.
2 Turkish infantry; c1900-40. This is

also found with arms as (1) and (4), and with second-quality painting dating from after 1922.
3 Egyptian infantry; c1900-40. This figure is also rarely found painted as East African Rifles in khaki.
4 West India Regiment; c1900-40. This is a head variation of the basic type and the earliest figure found with an alternative head.
5 Line infantry bugler; c1908. The first figure made by Baker, it has "BRITISH MAKE" on the leg. It was available in various paintings.
6 Fusilier; c1908. This is a head swap on the body of (5), also found as an officer, a bugler and at the slope arms. The painting was second-quality after 1922.
7-8 Indian infantry, and Italian Bersaglieri; c1922. This is the final-version marching figure,

which is found with many different heads and paintings. Alternative arms, one with a shovel being the rarest, are known. They were sold in boxes of eight, but without an officer.
9-16 Regimental band of the British Army, khaki service dress; c1921. Available as an eight-piece or 16-piece band, this figure (with different heads) was also catalogued in line infantry, Guards, steel helmet and US Army versions. Only one basic body is used for all the instrumentalists, the bass drum being wired to the body of the drummer and the side drum being held up by the two arms. This unfortunately did not result in one of Reka's best figures. The bands were later expanded by using a

figure standing at attention, first issued in 1920 for the Medical Corps set, in all the versions listed for the marching bands. Figures shown include: (9-16) fife player, tuba player, cornet player, cymbalist, side drummer, clarinettist, trombonist, and bass drummer. These figures are rare in all versions.
17 French infantry; c1915. This standing figure is also rarely found black-faced, possibly to portray a Moroccan.
18-19 Belgian infantry; c1915. Most makers painted French and Belgian uniforms on a common casting but Baker at least went to the trouble of issuing two different heads for the Belgian version. Of the two types the head used on (19) is the rarer.

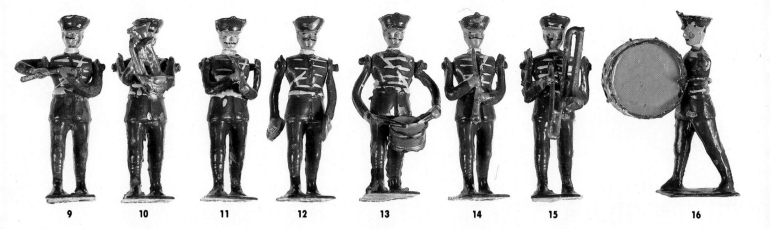

9 10 11 12 13 14 15 16

23 24 25 26 27 28 29

36 37 38 39 40

20 Territorial, full dress; c1914. Issued near the end of that year this casting became the basic firing body for over 20 heads.

21 Territorial, khaki service dress; c1914. An alternative paint style of (20), also found as USA (full dress and khaki) and Russian.

22 Indian infantry; c1914. Madras, Bombay and khaki uniforms are to be found on this figure, which is rarely found in good condition.

23 Indian Infantry; produced by Crescent, c1931. Cast from the (22) mould with the base marks erased, and with inferior painting.

24 Soldier in khaki, steel helmet; produced by Crescent, c1940. Cast from the same body mould as (23) this figure bears the Crescent trade-mark.

25 Scots Guard; c1910. A small

45mm (1.77in) standing firing figure, now rare, this was wholesaled mainly for use in Christmas crackers.

26, 27 Royal Navy bluejacket, and German sailor; maker unknown, probably post-1914. These figures, with a similar stance and identical arm (26) to figures (1-4), may have been made by the producer of Baker's figures from the early 1900s to 1908. They are square-based with no marks.

28 Charging Highlander; c1921. This rare item with a poorly-painted kilt is the only charging figure made by Reka to be found so far.

29 Marching Highlander; c1919. The first set to be issued after World War I, these Gordon Highlanders, again with a poor tartan, are rare.

30-31 Soldiers lying firing; c1915.

The popularity of standing and kneeling 1914 figures led to the unusual "back pack" lying sets. The line infantry and Guards are the most frequently found of the many variations, which included Australians and Gurkha Riflemen.

32 Soldier in khaki, kneeling firing; 1914. Rapidly introduced at the start of World War I this figure and its companion (standing at the ready with fixed bayonet) were cast from two-part moulds unsuitable for head-mould swapping. They were, however, painted as khaki "Tommies", red Territorials, blue Royal Marines, US and Russian soldiers, filling the gap until the more complex firing figures were ready.

33 Soldier in khaki, kneeling firing; c1916. The improved version of

(32), this figure was available in many different sets with various heads. See (34-40).

34 Soldier in khaki, wearing a foreign service helmet. c1916.

35 Foreign service, full dress; c1916. To this day red figures have an attractiveness which masks their lack of realism.

36 Prussian; c1916. Possibly as a result of poor sales, this figure has been painted (wrongly) as British line infantry.

37 Royal Scot; c1916. The most common firing Reka figure.

38 Lowland Scots Regiment; c1916.

39 Australian; c1916 — a cheap novelty gilt issue.

40 Italian Bersaglieri; produced by Crescent, c1946. This is a poorly painted common figure which is not often seen in its Reka form.

Reka mounted figures often bear a resemblance to some Britains items. This may be explained by the fact that George Wood, an ex-Britains toolmaker and co-founder of Johillco, was responsible for their design. In their Royal Army Medical Corps, Zulu and Naval figures, however, they display a style and originality which many consider equal to any Britains products of the same period. The high cost of the more complex mounted figures was again offset by interchangable head moulds and many different paintings. Most of the items illustrated are 54mm (2.12in) "standard" scale.

1 Life Guard; c1910. The most common Reka find, this fixed-arm figure has the trade mark clearly

visible on the saddle cloth and "BRITISH MAKE" just below it. The figure was sold in boxes of five and ten with an officer.
2 Life Guard officer; c1910. Until 1916 all Reka mounted officers were on white-painted horses even when, as in the case of Life Guards, this was incorrect.
3 Royal Horse Guards; c1910. A little less common than (1), this is also available in the same set make-up and with the same wrongly painted officer.
4 Life Guards officer; c1916. This is an improved figure with movable arm, on a correctly painted horse. The officer uses the same arm as the foot officer which accompanied figures (5-6) on *page 102*. The trade-marks now appear on the underside.

5 Dragoon trumpeter; c1916. Another gilt seaside souvenir, this figure was not sold until after World War I. It uses the same arm as the bugler at (5) *page 102*.
6 General officer; c1924. This movable-arm figure replaced one based on the style shown at (1-3). The same head mould was adapted for the new issue. It carries a different arm casting from the officer at (4) and this seems to have been used on all officers after this time.
7 Gilt cavalryman; c1910. The apparently fanciful combination of a bearskin head-dress and lance on this rare figure may have been prompted by a display of the Royal Scots Greys at the Royal Tournament in London, when they carried lances in a musical drive.

8 Life Guard; gilt, c1910. This rare figure has "REKA" and the name G. Wood on it. The similarity to (7) and (18) is apparent.
9 Hussar; gilt, c1916. The overlarge head on this figure is a feature common to all the various castings used with this horse. The movable arm with its carbine was used again on the later hussar (17), and by Crescent until 1956.
10-12 Royal Army Medical Corps; c1920. One of Reka's most attractive sets, the RAMC were sold in eight-piece and 24-piece sets which included stretcher bearers both walking and standing, doctors, and wooden-based tents with Red Cross flags as casualty dressing stations. The tents, wholesaled separately by Baker, are common but most of

4   5   6

10   11   12   13   14   15   16

20   21   22   23   24   25   26

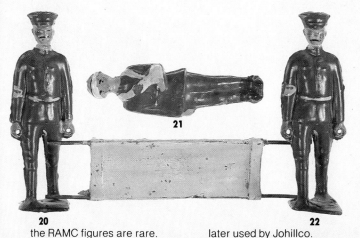

the RAMC figures are rare.
13 RAMC orderly with rolled
stretcher; c1920. An unusual
figure, part of the large set. The
movable arm with stretcher is
often missing. Also available in
khaki flat-cap form, as are all the
RAMC figures, this is the body
casting that is used for the
standing bandsmen.
14 RAMC sergeant; c1920. It is very
rare for NCOs to be depicted by
toy soldier makers except
occasionally in Colour Party and
Escort sets. As only one of these
was included in the large set this
is the rarest Reka RAMC figure.
15 Army Nursing Service; c1920.
Sold separately and in sets of
eight, this nurse is the most
common Reka RAMC figure. It
was the only mould known to be

later used by Johillco.
16 Zulu; c1921. This animated figure
was issued in the usual eight-
piece sets, and in a double set
box with eight of the charging
Highlanders shown at (28) *page
103*. It was later issued by
Crescent as a Maori war dancer!
It is scarce in both guises.
17 3rd Hussars, Royal Tournament;
c1921. Armed with a lance
instead of the usual carbine, this
figure formed part of the largest
Reka set depicting the popular
annual London event. Supplied in
a wooden box containing 86
pieces, the set comprised a band,
a gun team, sailors, cavalry and a
set-piece battle between firing
figures and Zulus.
18-19 Dragoons; c1914. Issued
before the outbreak of the war,

these bright figures contrast
strongly with the khaki reality of
later issues that year. A simple
fixed-arm casting, with its origins
in the small G. Wood figure (8)
clear to see, it was available
painted as every dragoon and
dragoon guard regiment in the
British Army. The officer is again
mounted on a white horse.
20-22 Royal Army Medical Corps,
active service dress; c1921. The
rare khaki version of the walking
stretcher party, these figures lack
the charm of the full dress sets
(10-14). The same ''wounded
soldier'' was apparently used in
both versions — as was the
nurse, but with a more sober grey
cloak around her shoulders. An
RAMC doctor figure in khaki has
not yet been found.

23 Royal Navy bluejacket, marching;
c1915. An excellent figure with
the true rolling gait of the ''Jack
Tar'', the sailor was pressed into
service in several sets. The
painting varied from full blue to
white-duck trousered, with white
tops, with caps or not as the
occasion demanded. The simple
insertion of a metal pin in the
hand part of the mould produced
a ''ring hand'' for landing parties.
24-26 Royal Navy field gun crew;
c1915. Identical figures to (23),
the only apparent difference is
the painting of gold cap band
flashes, and a small badge on the
arm of the petty officer (25).
These rare figures should be
considered genuine only if
accompanied by the complete
field gun display base or box.

After an inauspicious start as the Britannia Model Company during World War I — whereupon they were promptly sued by Johillco who had registered the Britannia Brand as a trade-mark — Soldarma blossomed to become perhaps the finest small manufacturer of well-made and animated toy figures. But despite an order from the King and Queen during the 1921 Royal Visit to the British Toy Fair, and a range of over 200 different sets by 1922, Soldarma were unable to survive the inter-war depression years, and ceased trading in 1933. The figures are mostly to 60mm (2.36in) scale, but considerable variety is found in the sets of "Tommies" in khaki — from 45mm (1.77in) to 70mm (2.75in).

1 Piper of the Scots Guards. With swinging plaid and flying pipe banners this figure is typical of the quality and animation to be found in the BMC series. Painted in all the Scots regiments' tartans it is one of the most common finds.
2 Gordon Highlander at the slope. These Scots are sometimes still found boxed in sets of eight, with a splendid label incorporating the famous Gale and Polden regimental postcard illustrations.
3 Royal Scots, marching with rifle slung. This is also found as the Kings Own Scottish Borderers.
4-5 Black Watch, marching at the trail. In common with most makers BMC used various arms to alter the appearance of the basic casting shown at (2).

6 London Scottish. From one of the earliest sets, this is perhaps the most successful fixed-arm marching figure by any maker.
7 12th Lancer. Again available painted in the uniform of most lancer regiments, this early model was issued in boxed sets of five and ten with an officer.
8 The Rifle Brigade. An unusual "scouting" figure of a rifleman, this is also (more rarely) found as a Kings Royal Rifle Corps version with red facing colours.
9 Royal Fusilier, kneeling to receive cavalry. The most commonly found BMC item, this figure is also found painted as a Danish Guard. It was reissued in plastic in the 1950s by an unknown manufacturer.
10 British cavalry in khaki. The large

solid horse made by BMC always looks capable of supporting its rider — unlike the spindly steeds produced by many other firms.
11 Imperial Russian infantry. Marching at the trail and slope as well as with slung rifle, this casting can be found, less often, painted as an Austrian.
12 Bulgarian infantry. Apart from Britains, BMC were one of the few companies to issue sets of the Balkan War armies.
13 Italian cavalry. This rare, colourful mounted set uses the same basic casting as (10). Being a fixed-arm figure the officer is distinguished by a red and gold edge to the saddlecloth instead of an extended sword arm.
14-15 Italian Bersaglieri. Marching at the slope and at the trail arms,

resplendent in their green
feathered hats, these two figures
form an interesting comparison
with the Fry and Reka models
shown on *page 98* and *page 102*.

16-17 French infantry, advancing
with fixed bayonets. This front
and back view shows the high
paint standard common to all
BMC figures throughout their
production. There does not
appear to have been any second-
quality "cheap line" painting as
was common to most other
British manufacturers at this time.

18-19 Belgian infantry, advancing
with fixed bayonets. Identical
castings to the French (16-17),
the popularity of these figures can
probably be gauged by their
frequence appearance —
although mint examples such as

these figures are now scarce.

20 British Army "Tommy", standing
firing. A "standard" 54mm
(2.12in) scale figure, this can be
identified by its diagonal stance
across its base. In common with
all BMC products it bears no
trade-mark or imprint.

21 British Army, lying firing. This
60mm (2.36in) scale figure can
also be found painted as a
Russian. Owing to the fragility of
the slender rifle barrel it is not
often discovered unbroken.

22 British Army, marching at the
slope. A 60mm (2.36in) scale
figure, this is the standard BMC
marching casting. It can be found
with a variety of heads and arms,
including this khaki flat-cap type.

23 British Army, Boer War. A 40mm
(1.57in) scale figure, also found in

a "full dress" painting of red and
blue, this was made for the
Christmas novelty cracker market
along with a small dustpan and
brush set. It is the "Holy Grail" for
BMC collectors.

24 British Army "Tommy". The
largest BMC figure found, this
scarce 70mm (2.75in) fixed-arm
soldier is reminiscent of classic
Western Front photographs of
tired but indomitable pipe-
smoking "regulars".

25 British Army, advancing with
fixed bayonet. Made to 45mm
(1.77in) scale this is again a
common find but often in poor
condition. It was sold in boxed
sets as well as singly, but these
only bear a simple label.

26 British Army cavalry officer. A
small 54mm (2.12in) scale figure,

this is perhaps one of BMC's least
attractive horses. The fixed-arm
troopers are rarer than the
officer, so this figure may have
been available in a variety of sets.

27 British Army, kneeling with fixed
bayonet. Fairly commonly found,
this is a head variation of (9).

28 British Army, Royal Horse Artillery,
seated gunner. Part of the gun
team shown on *pages 96-97*, this
was also issued as a Russian.

29 Imperial Russian artillery officer.
An imposing 60mm (2.36in) scale
figure on a thickset horse, this is
just a green-painted version of the
RHA officer. As it is more often
seen than any of the other
components of the gun teams it
may have been issued with other
sets. Scarce in this version, it is
very rare in the full RHA uniform.

Hollow-cast British Troops by John Hill & Co., UK

John Hill and Co., who are usually referred to by the name "Johillco" that appeared on many of their figures, were founded by a former employee of Britains, George Wood, *c*1900 and were regarded as their main rival.

1 An early peaked-cap lancer on a galloping horse, dated 23.10.1915. Normally found in khaki or gilt finish, this example is in "full dress" red tunic with dark blue cap and trousers.

2 Mounted Hussars, Large; no. 213A. This excellent figure has undergone some retouching and originally may not have had the red breeches of the 11th Hussars.

3 Hussar, mounted; no. 924. A fixed-arm figure, very inferior to (2), but in the 1930s it sold for two

pence rather than three!

4 Life Guard in cloak. Note the strong resemblance to the Britains piece — see (14) *page 38*.

5 A post-war Horse Guard, similar to the Britains figure at (11) *page 39*, although the saddle carbine is retained on the Johillco version.

6 12th Lancers (Prince of Wales Royal); no. 925. A movable-arm lancer on an indifferent horse.

7 Field marshall, mounted; no. 907. Included in many boxed sets, this is a late second-quality painting.

8 Dismounted general. A good casting, but in a second-grade finish. Originally this figure was available as no. 922: Senior Medical Officer.

9 Scots Greys trooper; no. 33P. Available in a number of sets, this and a number of other Johillco

Left: *Boxed sets of Johillco figures are quite hard to find; these are post-war examples. The "Zulus, ref. 259", are quite different figures from the first-version Johillco Zulus; the label is marked with a price of six shillings. The other set is "Scot prone ref. 122" — see (14) page 111. The price was six shillings and sixpence.*

cavalry use a horse very similar to a Britains second-grade figure, and one used by Reka.

10 Scots Greys standard-bearer; no. 692. A figure with "comic opera" epaulettes, his standard appears to be the Red Ensign of the British Merchant Navy!

11 The gilt version, no. 691G, of the Scots Greys trumpeter; no. 691. This is a quite attractive figure, on

a stubborn horse, but like (10) he has superfluous epaulettes.

12 A fixed-arm marching Guards officer with his hand on his sword hilt, a pose also used for the infantry officer (28 and 29).

13-14 Two paint versions of no. 215A, listed as a Scots Guardsman but here with the red plume of a Coldstream. (13) is a first-grade painting while (14) is a later, more basic paint job. They are movable-arm figures.

15 Scots Guards standard-bearer; no. 911. An early painting of this one-piece casting.

16 Firing Fusilier; no. 523C as a 1d line, and 523A as a 1½d line — this is presumably the former!

17 Grenadier Guard, kneeling firing. This would appear to be a later introduction than the kneeling

infantryman shown at (33).

18 Grenadier Guard, running; no. 243A. A movable-arm figure at the trail, similar to the Britains version but stepping off on the right rather than the left foot.

19-27 Johillco's only bandsmen are these nine Guardsmen, which were available singly, listed as Grenadier Guards. They were not sold as a complete boxed band, although items (19, 21, 22, 25 and 26) were listed as a Scots Guards band in set 38/5 — with other figures. It will be noted that these fixed-arm figures are painted as Coldstream Guards.

28 Marching infantry officer. This is the same as (12) but with a spiked helmet. It was originally available in dark blue as no. 923: Junior Medical Officer.

29 Marching infantry officer; as (28) but in a white helmet.

30 Liverpool Regiment (slope arms); no. 915C. A fixed-arm 1d figure.

31 Middlesex Regiment (Present Arms!); no. 910. The two arms and rifle are cast as a clip-on unit.

32 Firing Lincolnshire Regiment; no. 524A. The first-grade standing firing line infantryman.

33 Kneeling firing line infantryman, in a white helmet. In a blue helmet this was listed as no. 912: Manchester Regiment.

34 This line infantryman in spiked helmet standing at the ready is listed simply as 5d: Infantry, and was only available in second-grade finish.

35 Manchester Regiment, running; no. 245A. This is the same as (18) but with a spiked helmet.

Hollow-cast British and European Troops by John Hill & Co., UK

1 Fusilier (Attention!); no. 909C.
2 Inniskilling Fusilier, Marching; Johillco no. 689.
3 Royal Welch Fusiliers goat mascot handler. An item which Britains never produced.
4 Goat mascot. A re-use of Johillco's farm goat.
5-6 Highland officers. A late 1930s fixed-arm figure (5) and a similar post-war officer with a movable sword arm (6). Johillco tartans tend to be vague and/or garish.
7 Black Watch, Marching; no. 244A. A movable-arm Highlander with correct red hackle, but extraneous yellow on his kilt.
8 A Highland piper in glengarry; Johillco no. 215P.
9-10 Royal Scots. A fixed-arm officer (9) and movable-arm private (10).

11 An overscale Black Watch Highlander, at the ready.
12 Black Watch charging; no. 908.
13 Kneeling Highlander; no. 11AC.
14 Prone Highlander; no. 12AC.
15-16 Royal Canadian Mounted Police. Available together in several boxed sets, and separately as no. 773 mounted, and no. 918 on foot.
17 Cavalry, service dress; no. 535A.
18 Officer, Khaki (fixed-arm); 451C.
19 Marching Infantry, Khaki; no. 594C. This World War I British infantryman has knee boots rather than puttees.
20 Drummer, Khaki; no. 13D.
21 Bugler, Khaki; no. 13B. A good pose, but somewhat over-sized.
22 This infantryman, in equipment of the 1903-8 period, should pre-date (19), but oddly it is always

found in a late-version painting.
23 Another oddity: close examination of this British soldier reveals him to be a re-use of the Ethiopian infantryman (see *page 11*) complete with bare feet!
24 A British World War I infantryman throwing a stick grenade. He is dated 1915.
25 Firing Infantry, Khaki; no. 10A.
26 A kneeling machine-gunner, in service uniform; no. 614P. An attractive and common figure.
27 This kneeling sepoy is one of the more elusive Johillco pieces.
28 Charging Australian infantryman — one of Johillco's best poses.
29 Kneeling machine-gunner, service uniform; no. 614P.
30 This unusual version of (31) *page 109* would appear to be in the Artillery or Ordnance Corps.

31 Royal Navy bluejacket, standing at the ready; in a first-quality early paint finish.
32 Royal Navy bluejacket, kneeling to receive cavalry.
33-34 Marching bluejackets at the trail and at the slope; late 1930s.
35 US Navy whitejacket. A completely different, post-war figure for export.
36 US Marine. A post-war figure, probably also intended for export.
37 An unusual early Austrian soldier in shako and double-breasted tunic, dated 1911.
38 Russian infantryman. This scarce figure is the same casting as (19) in a dark green uniform.
39 Japanese infantryman. This is the companion to the Russian (38) and is also based on (19).
40 Greek Evzone. This interesting

110

10   11   12   13   15   16

14

24   25   26   27   28

42   29

39   40   41   43   44   45   46   47   48

Left: *Johillco produced a small range of under-scale vehicles. Most of these were close copies of the US Tootsie Toy range, including the tank, no. 604, based on a Renault vehicle. Alongside it is an unusual Tank Corps man, also rather undersized. On the right is the howitzer, no. 621C. The despatch rider on motorcycle, no. 591D, has a detachable rider and revolving wheels. The battledress figures, introduced post-war, have holes in their left hands to accept a Bren gun, pick-axe shovel or rifle.*

fixed-arm marching figure is more usually found in a red jacket.

41-42 Stretcher bearer and casualty (full dress uniform). These are quite scarce items; the casualty is

a "full dress" painting of the Ethiopian wounded figure.

43 Standing nurse. This is a re-issue of the nurse by Reka shown at (15) page 105.

44 Doctor, Service Dress; no. 682. This is a re-use of the guard from the railway series, minus his flag!

45 A steel-helmeted soldier dragging his wounded comrade from the battlefield.

46 A member of the Home Guard, also available as an airman — see (7) page 64.

47 A rare figure from c1939 of a soldier in full anti-gas equipment. The object on his bayonet represents a gas detector, which would change colour in the presence of gas.

48 Gunner in gas mask; no. 943. There was also a kneeling figure.

1 Marching GI; by Charbens. This is from a series similar in style to the Timpo range shown at (16-27) *page 115*, but identifiable by their rimless pot-shaped helmets.

2 A movable-arm lancer, produced *c*1950 by Cherilea.

3 An ATS or Women's Army figure, at "eyes left"; by Cherilea.

4 A post-war prone firing Highlander, by Crescent.

5 Kneeling firing Highlander in tropical helmet; no. 197 by Crescent.

6-9 British battledress infantry by Crescent, introduced *c*1939.

10-11 This wireless operator, (with detachable "diamond" aerial) and field telephone operator by Crescent were available together in set K703: Field Wireless Set.

12 Steel-helmeted Highlander throwing a grenade, by Crescent.

13 This Crescent figure wearing a greatcoat is usually found as an airman — see (32) *page 65* — but in khaki he may be a British soldier or US airman.

14 Dismounted Life Guard, made in the 1950s by Crescent.

15 A fixed-arm Highlander, no. A213 by Crescent.

16 An unusual Indian Army lancer produced by Crescent in the 1950s. This is one of the few pieces to have the crescent moon logo of the firm on the belly of the horse; the wire lance is cast in.

17 A kneeling nurse with bandage; no. A28 by Crescent.

18 The rather undersized Crescent standing nurse, no. A180.

19 Womens Auxiliary Territorial Service with steel helmet; Crescent no. A88. See *page 14*.

20 A cutlass-wielding bluejacket, Crescent no. 208, available before World War II.

21 This naval officer with telescope (the end of which is missing) is listed as A219: Midshipman.

22 Zulu warrior; Crescent no. A162.

23 Arab warrior with a scimitar. Crescent no. A181.

24 Abyssinian; Crescent no. A23.

25-26 US Marine Corps; by Crescent. These figures were produced in the 1950s, probably for export.

27-28 Royal Canadian Mounted Police; by Crescent, 1950s.

29 Highland piper in feather bonnet; by the Fylde Manufacturing Co. Note that apart from the head this is virtually identical to the Johillco piper at (8) *page 110*.

30 Black Watch Highlander, with

7 8 9 10 11 12 13

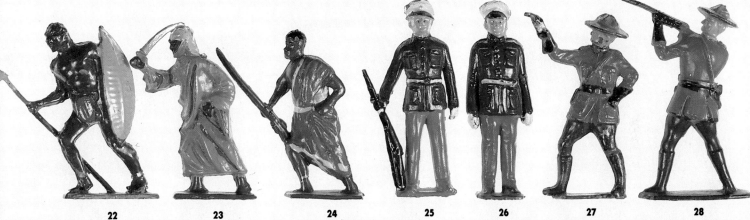

22 23 24 25 26 27 28

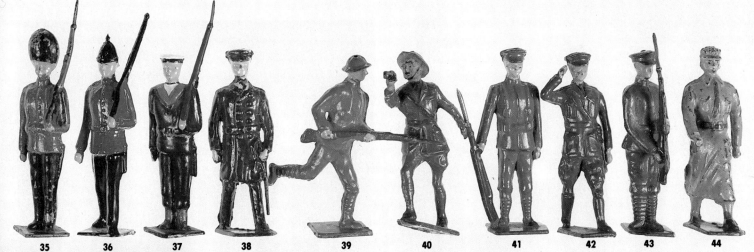

35 36 37 38 39 40 41 42 43 44

Left: *On the left: from Cherilea's "Baronial Series", Edward the Black Prince. To a better standard than their usual figures, the Black Prince is removable from his horse and has an optional sword or battle axe (not shown) to place in his hand. On the right is Crescent's set 700: Royal Engineers Field Telephone. It has two identical service dress figures; to the back of one is clipped a spool of copper wire. The other figure pays out the "cable" to a telegraph pole.*

movable arm; by the firm of M.S.R. (1950-53) whose only other figures appear to have been a Household Cavalry trooper and a Grenadier Guardsman.
31 Kew or Ku-zu models, active

between the wars, are best known for their charming farm and village items, but they did produce this attractive khaki stretcher party unit which is also found in dark blue.
32-34 The small firm of H.R. Products (H. Reynolds) produced some sturdy Vikings (32 and 34) and some positively fat Romans (33) as well as a "Treasure Island" range in the 1950s.
35-44 Taylor & Barrett Ltd are probably best known to collectors for their range of vehicles and civilian items, but they produced some attractive military figures, sometimes slightly under-sized, as shown by the rest of the figures on this page.
35 Guardsman at attention.
36 Marching line infantryman at

the slope, in a late painting.
37 Bluejacket at attention, slope arms. Note that T. & B. figures at attention and at the present have diamond-shaped bases.
38 An attractive figure of a naval officer marching in a frock coat.
39 Charging British World War I infantryman, in steel helmet.
40 World War I British officer, advancing with pistol.
41 Khaki peaked-cap World War I infantryman, standing at ease.
42 World War I British officer, saluting. The sword scabbard is broken on this example.
43 Khaki peaked-cap infantryman, presenting arms.
44 A sturdy ATS figure by Taylor & Barrett; it will be noted that she has broader shoulders than any of the men produced by that firm.

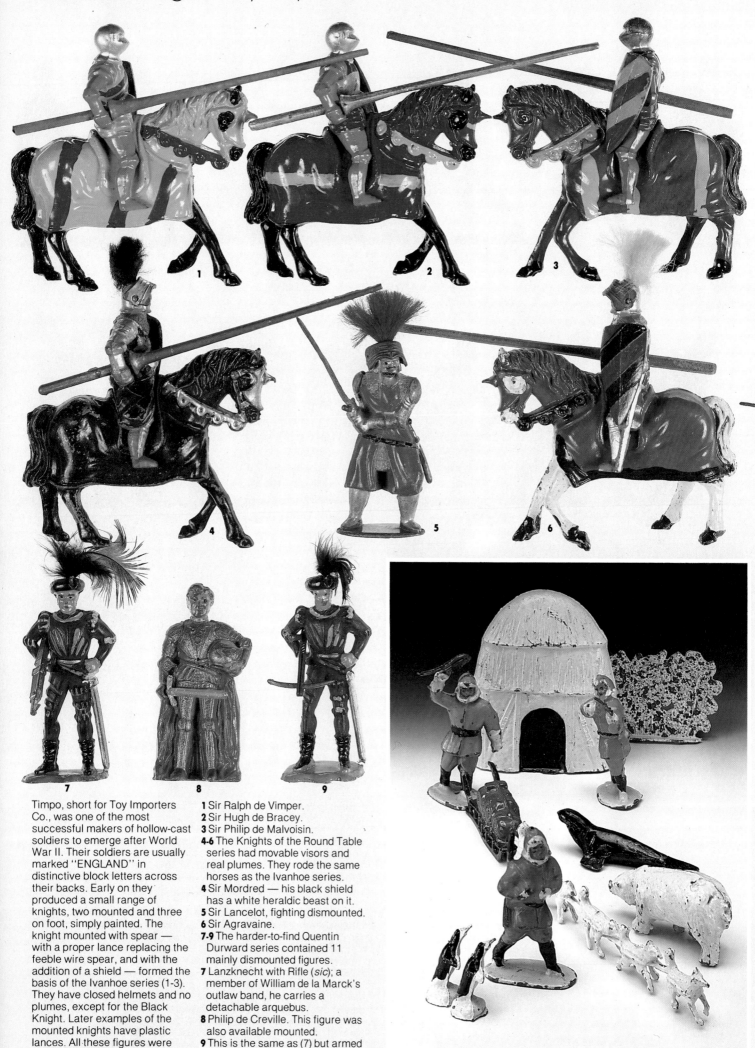

Timpo, short for Toy Importers Co., was one of the most successful makers of hollow-cast soldiers to emerge after World War II. Their soldiers are usually marked "ENGLAND" in distinctive block letters across their backs. Early on they produced a small range of knights, two mounted and three on foot, simply painted. The knight mounted with spear — with a proper lance replacing the feeble wire spear, and with the addition of a shield — formed the basis of the Ivanhoe series (1-3). They have closed helmets and no plumes, except for the Black Knight. Later examples of the mounted knights have plastic lances. All these figures were sold individually boxed.

1 Sir Ralph de Vimper.
2 Sir Hugh de Bracey.
3 Sir Philip de Malvoisin.
4-6 The Knights of the Round Table series had movable visors and real plumes. They rode the same horses as the Ivanhoe series.
4 Sir Mordred — his black shield has a white heraldic beast on it.
5 Sir Lancelot, fighting dismounted.
6 Sir Agravaine.
7-9 The harder-to-find Quentin Durward series contained 11 mainly dismounted figures.
7 Lanzknecht with Rifle (sic); a member of William de la Marck's outlaw band, he carries a detachable arquebus.
8 Philip de Creville. This figure was also available mounted.
9 This is the same as (7) but armed with a crossbow.

Left: *One of the earliest offerings from Timpo was their Arctic set. This came in several different permutations, but most of the elements are shown here. The presence of both penguins and a docile looking polar bear must throw the explorers into some confusion as to which polar region they are in. One explorer takes aim at the savage fauna, which also includes a seal, while another trudges on with slung rifle. The third member of the team cracks his whip over a team of willing but tiny huskies all cast in one piece, like a lead caterpillar, which haul a well-modelled, if undersized sledge. The Arctic wastes are conveyed by a snow-covered bush and a white-painted African hut masquerading as an igloo.*

10-15 Timpo's two largest series were their West Point Cadets and US Army and Navy series. The West Point Cadet range had 20 different figures.
10 Cadet tuba player; no. 7007.
11 Bugler; no. 7004.
12 Trombone player; no. 7006.
13 Side drummer; no. 7002.
14 Mounted officer; no. 7016. Detachable, he uses the same horse as the Timpo British mounted policeman.
15 Cadet at ease; no. 7013.
16-31 The US Army and Navy series contained over 30 different items and is generally considered to be the best range of World War II toy soldier GIs produced. Both these figures and the West Point Cadets were later issued in plastic.
16 Charging US Infantry; no. 9013.

17 Firing Kneeling Infantry; no. 9018 in the series.
18 Officer; no. 9009.
19 Firing Standing Infantry; no. 9011. Note that this is an interesting variation by Timpo painted as a black soldier.
20 Washing; no. 9023. A nice domestic touch!
21 Eating; no. 9026. This figure also has a mug of coffee in his hand.
22 Military Police; no. 9032.
23 Wounded; Walking, no. 9025. A well-modelled figure with bandaged head and arm in sling.
24 Infantryman at Ease; no. 9000.
25 Infantryman Marching; no. 9001. This interesting figure appears to be going on leave or changing camp, as he carries his pack in his left hand.
26 Ceremonial, Marching; no. 9020.

This figure is in service dress and wearing an overseas cap.
27 Ceremonial Officer; no. 9022. Empty-handed in service dress and overseas cap.
28 British soldiers in khaki, no. 7: officer. Timpo's British soldiers in battledress never seem to have been as popular as the GIs; the series only ran to 10 figures, of which this is the commonest.
29 Naval Officer; no. 9030. Although listed in the US Army and Navy series, this is really a Royal Navy officer.
30 Sailor on Guard; no. 9029. This is also in reality a Royal Navy bluejacket.
31 Sailor; no. 8009. A Royal Navy sailor on leave with his kitbag on his shoulder, from the model railways figures range.

Between the wars the firm of Comet Metal Products of New York produced a range of undistinguished 55mm (2.16in) solid lead soldiers. After World War II, one Curt Wennberg — a Swedish Naval Attache in the USA — helped gain the services of the Swedish designer Holger Eriksson. Taking advantage of an Irish Government subsidy, Comet set up a factory in Galway to produce Eriksson's designs under the name "Authenticast". This international arrangement was not without its difficulties, culminating in a fire in 1950 which put an end to the Irish factory. Most Authenticast figures are marked "Eire" and "HE" for Holger Eriksson, although a few pieces have other initials. Most,

but not all, of the striding figures have a cruciform base.

1 17th-century pikeman, steadying his pike while drawing his sword.
2 French Napoleonic infantryman, of an Italian regiment, advancing.
3 French Napoleonic line infantry officer, in bicorne hat.
4 French "Turco" or tirailleur of c1900, at the charge.
5 Franco-Prussian War Franc-tireur; a different painting of an American Civil War figure.

Right: An example of a boxed set of Authenticast figures: the Franc-tireurs as mentioned at (5). Note the motto: "The finest models ever built". The word "Gaeltacht" refers to the Gaelic-speaking part of western Ireland.

20   **21**   **22**   **23**   **24**

25   **26**   **27**   **28**   **29**   **30**

31   **32**   **33**   **34**   **35**   **36**

6 Franco-Prussian War French line infantryman, in an interesting "on guard" stance.

7-8 Chasseur à Pied (Light Infantry) officer and man, c1870, marching.

9-10 Zouave, with impressively piled pack (9), and an officer (10) which is a different painting of (8).

11 Indian Army sepoy, at ease.

12-13 British line infantry of 1900, at attention. These figures are not by Eriksson, being marked "L.N." on the base. The officer (12) is an adaptation of the man: the soldered-on rifle has been left off, a sheathed sword added, and a sash painted on.

14 Marching Royal Marine.

15 World War I British officer, in trenchcoat, equipped with binoculars and map case.

16 World War I British soldier; an evocative figure "standing to" in steel helmet and greatcoat.

17 French Army officer of 1939, in khaki service dress with a swagger-stick under his arm.

18 World War II British soldier, in shorts and slung rifle.

19 Swiss Guard of the Vatican, in undress uniform with rifle.

20-30 With the failure of the Irish factory Comet continued producing soldiers in New York while Wennberg moved to South Africa and set up the Swedish African Engineers, known as SAE.

20 Ancient Teuton warrior, with braided hair and arm rings.

21 A rather small Viking with shield and long sword.

22 Ancient Egyptian foot soldier, with spear and shield.

23 Ancient Egyptian officer, with plumed head-dress and sword.

24 Portuguese infantryman, of the Napoleonic period.

25 Indian Army sepoy, in khaki with red facings.

26 French Turco, charging. Compare with the figure at (4).

27 Italian Bersaglieri, prone firing, an unusual portrayal in British-type post-war battledress.

28 World War II British soldier, in shirt sleeves, running at the trail.

29 World War I German infantry officer, charging with pistol.

30 A post-war British Guardsman, in stiff peaked cap, battledress and blancoed webbing.

31-32 The Japanese firm of Minikins, active in the 1950s, are usually regarded as merely pirates of other firms' work, but they did in fact produce some interesting original pieces including this Japanese samurai and 17th-century soldier with early firearm.

33-36 In 1935 the Belgian Emmanuel Steinback introduced his range of quality figures under the name MIM (Maximus In Minimus). Ancients, Napoleonics and some contemporary figures were produced, the size being 60mm (2.35in). They are readily identifiable by the beautifully designed bases which are marked underneath "MIM" with a coat of arms and a brief description of the figure.

33 Syrian warrior, with a sling.

34 Ancient Egyptian warrior.

35 Roman centurion, with his vine branch staff of office.

36 Roman legionary, carrying a pilum and shield.

American and Canadian "Dimestore" Figures

1
2
3
4
5
6

14
15
16
17

22
23
24
25
26
27

The USA relied mainly on imports until the 1920s, when a number of toy soldier makers commenced production. Of these, the large 3¼-inch hollow-casts by Barclay, Manoil and others, produced in the 1930s, are very collectable.

1-3 These figures were included in a "military display tray" game by C.W. Beiser's American Soldier Co. of New York. C.W. Beiser was the inventor of the game, discussed on *page 78*. In Spanish-American War (1898) uniform, these figures may have been produced by the American Soldier Co. themselves, but more likely by an outside firm such as Barclay.
1 Artilleryman with rammer.
2 Mounted officer, riding a rearing brown horse.

3 Infantryman at the ready.
4-6 The Ideal Toy Co. of Bridgeport, Connecticut, produced 54mm (2.12in) hollow-casts in the 1920s, using moulds from Germany:
4 Officer, with movable sword arm.
5 Bugler, with the same body as (4).
6 A fixed-arm US sailor with rifle.
7 World War I US infantryman. This 40mm (1.57in) figure is from the "Uncle Sam's Defenders" series introduced by the Grey Iron Casting Co. in the early 1930s. One of the few firms to make toy soldiers in cast iron, they had previously produced a range of nickel-plated figures of the same size in 1898 period uniforms, and in 1933 introduced figures in the 3¼-inch "Dime Store Size".
8-11 John Lloyd Wright, the son of Frank Lloyd Wright the architect,

made toys under several trade names, including Lincoln Log. From 1929 to World War II a small range of solid-cast civilian and military figures was produced.
8 US infantryman, in the uniform of Wayne's Legion, 1794.
9 Marching US infantryman of 1918. The top of the rifle is missing in this example.
10 Mounted US officer of 1918.
11 Charging US infantryman, 1918.
12-13 The Canadian toy soldier trade has always relied principally on imports from the UK — chiefly of Britains — and from the USA, except in time of war when outside supplies were cut off. During World War II the firm of London Toy produced a range of vehicles and some military figures cast at attention, such as this pilot

(12), and airman of the Royal Canadian Air Force (13).
14-30 The term "Dime Store soldiers" is almost synonymous with the names of Barclay and Manoil, who both started producing hollow-cast figures in the early 1930s. Dime Store figures tend to be individualists going about different tasks, rather than marching in formation. Barclays can be distinguished by separate tin helmets — until World War II when cast helmets came in — and a distinctive way of painting the eyes with a curved eybrow and dot shown clearly on (22). Manoil are normally marked as such, and compared to Barclay figures they have a more sculptural quality and are often more inventive in their poses.

14 ''Long stride'' naval officer; Barclay 721.

15 Soldier, releasing carrier pigeons; Barclay 731.

16 ''Short stride'' standing firing infantryman; Barclay 747.

17 Kneeling machine-gunner; Barclay 702, an early figure.

18 Radio operator, with separate aerial; Barclay 951.

19 One of several versions of a searchlight and operator, cast as one piece; Barclay 776.

20 Doctor; Barclay 760.

21 A Manoil nurse of formidable aspect.

22 A Barclay skier of 1940, no. 785.

23 Sailor, in white uniform; Barclay 919; in the style known as ''pod foot'' produced in the 1950s.

24 ''Pod foot'' officer; Barclay 908.

25 ''Pod foot'' soldier equipped with slung rifle; Barclay 988.

26 ''Pod foot'' soldier with flame-thrower; Barclay 991.

27 ''Pod foot'' soldier charging; Barclay 906.

28 Machine-gunner; Barclay 928.

29 Observer; Manoil 526. This is a post-war figure.

30 Motorcycle rider; Manoil 529. A post-war figure.

Right: *Both Manoil and Barclay also produced vehicles and equipment but this was undersized in relation to their soldiers. Shown here are two Manoil tractors, hauling a field kitchen and water cart, and a caisson (limber) and field gun. These are in fact re-casts, from the original moulds, by Ron Eccles of Burlington, Iowa.*

Composition Figures by Elastolin, Lineol and other Makers

Composition figures are made from a mixture of sawdust, casein glue and kaolin, pressed into a brass mould around a wire armature and "cooked" at a moderate temperature. This technique for producing soldiers has been used in a number of continental European countries, and in the United Kingdom and the USA when wartime shortages made lead unobtainable. But it reached its finest form in the excellent figures of the two German firms Hausser-"Elastolin" and Lineol. The main problem with composition figures is that of damp. If moisture reaches the wire armature corrosion sets in, resulting in splitting and deterioration of the whole figure.

1-9 Elastolin figures of the post-war West German Army or "Bundeswehr", produced in the 1950s. These are based on pre-war German Army figures, but with American-style helmets: (1) standing firing infantryman — compare with (32); (2) cavalryman with slung rifle; (3) advancing officer; (4) side drummer; (5) bass drummer; (6) clarinettist; (7) trombone player; (8) French horn player; (9) tuba player.

10-17 These approximately 100mm (4in) tall figures by Elastolin were dropped from the catalogue by 1936 as the company concentrated on their enormous range of the German armed forces in 70mm (2.75in) and 40mm (1.57in) sizes. They are: (10) Indian Army sepoy; (11)

French Army Zouave; (12) French Army Algerian Tirailleur; (13-17) marching Guardsmen; (13) officer with tin sword; (14) standard-bearer; (15) side drummer; (16-17) Guardsmen.

18-19 German officer and infantryman, produced by Elastolin in the early 1930s before the introduction of Nazi insignia.

20 Sailor with side drum, an unusual musician figure produced in Portugal, c1960.

21 Signallers with morse key. One of Hausser-Elastolin's ingenious accessories, this working morse key has the morse code printed on a hinged tin plate which flips up from under the base. This is a post-war example of an item introduced in the late 1930s.

22-23 Officer and man of the Gordon

Highlanders, by Elastolin, 65mm (2.56in) high.

24 British infantryman, prone firing. A German infantryman with a change of head, he also incorporates a mechanism to delight a child of any age. A trap-door in the underside can be opened to cock a spring-loaded hammer and place an amorce cap in position. Prod the prone figure in the back and an explosion results! See also (32).

25 Walking nurse; by a Belgian firm, marked "Fabrication Belge".

26 Walking wounded; by Elastolin, with bandaged head and foot.

27 Kneeling nurse; by Elastolin. This particular example was produced after World War II.

28 Field kitchen; from an extensive range of vehicles, both horse-

drawn and motorized, by Elastolin. This typically German Army piece of equipment is shown here in the British version with small-size British soldiers. It was also available with larger German Army figures. Note the wheeled bases to the draught horses — a rather antiquated traditional toy feature. See (33).

29 SA Brown Shirt or Storm Trooper; by Lineol. Elastolin, Lineol and several minor firms made many Nazi Party figures — now relatively scarce because of a ban on their possession in the immediate post-war period.

30 SS standard-bearer, by Froma. The standard is missing.

31 German infantryman; a figure of unknown make.

32 A standing firing German

infantryman, by Elastolin. A spring mechanism in the backpack fires a cap, producing a loud report and a puff of smoke from the hollow gun barrel.

33 Horse-drawn ambulance, by Elastolin, in tinplate with cloth awnings; like (28) it has a rather undersized British crew.

34 World War I British or American officer in steel helmet, by Lineol.

35 Italian Bersaglieri; by Lineol, based on a German infantryman but with the distinctive headgear.

36 World War I British infantryman in peaked cap, by Lineol. This is a specially designed figure.

37 Belgian Army standard-bearer of c1914; a small-size figure produced by Elastolin.

38 French World War I soldier in tunic; by Lineol, and based on a

German Army figure.

39 French Army signaller with notepad; by Lineol.

40-42 Three post-war personality figures by Durso: (40) Stalin; (41) Tito and (42) Eisenhower. These are 80mm (3.15in) tall.

43 Field Marshall von Hindenberg, in greatcoat and peaked cap; produced by Elastolin.

44 Field Marshall von Hindenberg, in World War I uniform; by Lineol.

45 Belgian Army officer, in French-type "Adrian" helmet and khaki uniform; by Elastolin, to 54mm (2.12in) scale.

46-47 British Army World War I bugler and infantryman; by Elastolin, 54mm (2.12in) scale.

48 Mounted figure of Frederick the Great of Prussia, by Elastolin.

49 Prussian infantry officer, saluting

with his "spontoon" or pike, produced by Elastolin.

50-51 Marching Prussian Grenadiers; by Elastolin. (51) is at the "eyes right" position.

52 One of Elastolin's finest pieces: a signaller releasing a carrier pigeon while his alsatian dog looks on. Originally produced as a German Army figure, this is a "neutralised" version in the distinctive Swiss Army helmet, produced post-war.

53 Prone heavy machine-gunner, in post-war Swiss Army guise; produced by Elastolin.

54 Marching Swiss infantryman; produced by Elastolin.

55 Swiss infantryman; by Elastolin. A later post-war version specially designed with an open-collared tunic and full trousers.

Aluminium would at first seem an unpromising material from which to produce toy soldiers, but once cast it has the advantages of lightness and durability without the toxic hazards associated with lead. The French were the main exponents of aluminium figures, with firms such as Quiralu in the 1930s producing pleasing results. The only large-scale producer of aluminium figures in the UK was Wend-Al of Blandford, Dorset who set up just after World War II with the assistance of Quiralu. They were at first quite successful, but post-war economic restrictions and the appearance of plastic figures in the early 1950s brought about the end of aluminium figure production in 1956.

Aluminium figures were made by a sand-casting technique, the master being a plate with raised detail for a dozen or so figures on both sides. Sand was beaten down on to each half of the plate, which was then carefully removed and the two sand mould halves brought together. Molten aluminium was poured into the channels leading into each cavity; when the sand was brushed off, a network of sprues linking a series of figures was left, like a modern plastic kit. The figures were removed from the sprues, "fettled" (cleaned of superfluous metal) and painted. This process obviously demanded some care if a good figure was to be produced. Quiralu produced a crisp and pleasingly detailed figure, but towards the end Wend-Al's figures lacked this quality. Items (1-10) are by Quiralu, the remainder by Wend-Al. They are generally slightly over 54mm (2.12in) "standard" size.

1-3 Officer, soldier and bugler of the Algerian Tirailleurs or "Turcos".
4 St. Cyr cadet, from the French officer training school.
5 French sailor, in blue uniform.
6-7 French sailors, in white uniform, one marching at the slope, and one blowing a bugle.
8 A scarce figure of a jet pilot produced by Quiralu.
9-10 "Toy Soldier" figures in Napoleonic style uniform.
11-17 These Quiralu designs were issued by Wend-Al as their "Toy Town" range, attired in British red jackets and blue trousers.
11 Listed by Wend-Al as a nurse, this battered figure is really a *cantiniere* (a uniformed camp follower who supplied refreshments to the troops).
12 Soldier, saluting with musket.
13 Fife player.
14 Drummer.
15-16 Late-production Wend-Al versions of (9) and (10). Note the more basic painting compared with (12-14).
17 The charming mounted officer on his rocking horse.
18 Royal Canadian Mounted Policeman.
19 Life Guard. This figure was also available as a Horse Guard.
20 H.M. Queen Elizabeth II, riding side-saddle in uniform as Colonel-in-Chief of the Guards.

9 ... **10** ... **11** ... **12** ... **13** ... **14** ... **15** ... **16**

21 ... **22** ... **23** ... **17**

33

31 ... **32** ... **34** ... **35** ... **36** ... **37** ... **38** ... **39** ... **40**

21 Trumpeter, from the mounted band of the Life Guards.

22 12th Lancer officer.

23 Dismounted Life Guard, also produced as a Horse Guard.

24 Desert patrol trooper and camel, based on the French Saharan troops. This man rides a furry flock-coated camel!

25 Kneeling firing modern soldier, very similar to a Herald figure.

26 Soldier advancing with sub-machine gun.

27-34 Wend-Al Coldstream Guards: (27) early pattern with tall plume; (28) the most commonly-found type; (29) another version, similar to a Timpo figure; (30) standard-bearer with paper flag, which replaced an earlier one in tin; (31) a version of (29) with a flocked bearskin; (32) officer with wire

sword and flocked bearskin; (33) lying firing guardsman with flocked bearskin; (34) bass drummer with flocked bearskin, from a Guards band.

35-36 Highlanders, kneeling and standing firing, in feather bonnets and painted as Gordons.

37 Scots piper, produced in various paint finishes.

38 Marching Highlander; the most common type, generally found in Black Watch tartan.

39 Marching Highlander, a final version figure.

40 Highlander; the first version, of French design.

Left: *An officer and man of the Chasseurs Alpins on skis, by Quiralu. They have tinplate skis, and originally had wire ski poles.*

Plastic Figures by Various Makers

Plastic toy soldiers have been generally looked down on by collectors in the past, but interest in them is now growing.

1 American Civil War Confederate officer; by Elastolin, c1980.

2 Mounted Wehrmacht officer; by Elastolin, c1980.

3 Swiss infantryman; by Elastolin, c1980.

4 American Civil War Union infantryman, kneeling; by Elastolin, c1980.

5-6 Modern Austrian Army standard-bearer with metal flag, and bugler; by Elastolin.

7 Swiss infantryman marching, eyes right; produced by the French firm of Starlux.

8 Swiss dragoon; by Starlux.

9-10 Dutch Grenadiers: standard-bearer and marching at the slope; by Walter Merten of West Berlin.

11 Modern East German soldier; of unknown make.

12-13 Modern West German soldiers; by Walter Merten.

14 Ski trooper; by Reamsa, a prolific but now defunct Spanish firm.

15 Spanish sailor; by Reamsa.

16-19 Figures by the contemporary Greek firm Athena: (16) paratrooper at the slope; (17) sailor with Greek flag; (18) airman standing at ease; (19) mounted army officer.

20-37 The Britains "Eyes Right" series, a range of full dress plastic figures with movable heads and arms, was brought out in the 1960s. The examples illustrated are: (20) Life Guard trooper; (21) Horse Guard trooper; (22) Life Guard kettle drummer from the mounted band; (23) Life Guard trombone player from the mounted band; (24) US Army band clarinet player; (25) US Army band side drummer; (26) US Army band drum major; (27) US Army band French horn player; (28) US marine marching at the slope; (29) US marine colour-bearer with national standard; (30) US marine officer with sword at the carry; (31) US marine colour-bearer with Marine Corps colour; (32) US marine sloping arms on the left (only used with the colour party); (33) Royal Canadian Mounted Policeman; (34) private of the Middlesex Regiment in 1900s full dress; (35) Scots Guards piper; (36) Scots Guardsman marching at shoulder arms; (37) Scots Guards officer.

38-47 Figures by Reissler of Denmark: (38) Women's Army figure of original design; (39) airman of original design; (40) observer with binoculars — a copy of the Timpo figure; (41) infantryman with a sub-machine-gun based on a Timpo figure; (42) A sentry box in hard plastic; (43) Life Guard at present arms; (44) four Life Guards marching at the slope; (45) Life Guard officer; (46) Life Guard standard bearer; (47) Life Guard side drummer.

48-57 Figures from the excellent Herald range, which became part of Britains in 1958: (48) Guardsman at ease; (49) Guards officer; (50) Guards colour bearer; (51) Gordon Highlander side drummer; (52) Gordon Highlander

bass drummer; (53) Gordon Highlander drum major; (54) Gordon Highlander piper; (55) Horse Guard standard-bearer; (56) Life Guard standard-bearer; (57) an early fixed-arm version of the khaki infantryman at attention.

58-65 British infantry by Herald in the uniform of the early 1950s. The figures are: (58) grenade thrower; (59) advancing infantryman; (60) firing infantryman; (61) radio operator; (62) wounded infantryman; (63) officer; (64) charging infantryman; (65) kneeling firing infantryman.

66-70 "Enemy Infantry" produced by Herald in the early 1960s. These are the same as (58-65), in grey.

71-72 Two Highlanders at ease, in tropical helmet and feather bonnet, by Malleable Mouldings.

These are rare examples of figures produced by a short-lived British firm that pioneered plastic soldiers from 1947-50.

73 World War I British cavalry trumpeter; from a short-lived range by Crescent, c1960.

74 A bemedalled Guardsman and sentry box; by Kentoys, who produced a small range of figures in the late 1950s, some of them very similar to Herald items.

75-81 A surprising variety of soldiers are produced in Poland. Shown here are: (75) Polish cavalry trooper of 1939; (76) Polish cavalry trumpeter of 1939; (77) King Jan Sobieski; (78) modern Polish paratrooper; (79) Napoleonic infantryman standing at attention; (80) Polish revolutionary of 1830; (81)

medieval crossbowman.

82-87 In the mid-1960s the firm of Mini Models brought out a range of hard plastic figures, with detachable soft plastic headgear. These depicted World War II American, German and Japanese troops, plus a machine-gun, mortar and pack mule. The figures illustrated are: (82) Japanese soldier charging; (83) Japanese soldier kneeling firing; (84) German soldier marching; (85) German soldier standing firing; (86) American soldier throwing grenade; (87) American soldier charging.

88-89 A pair of unusual Turkish-made figures: (88) mounted standard-bearer with paper flag; (89) an infantryman from the same set, but to a larger scale.

90-93 In the late 1950s Britains produced a small, short-lived range of English Civil War figures. (90) Roundhead trooper; (91) Roundhead pikeman; (92) Cavalier trooper; (93) Cavalier musketeer.

94 Dismounted knight advancing with bill, from the Britains-Herald "Swoppet" range. These amazing figures had interchangeable crests and weapons, opening visors, and swords which could be drawn from their metal scabbards.

95-96 Kneeling and standing firing modern British Army figures from a small "Swoppet" range.

97 Britains Mini Set 1071: US Machine-gun Crew. This is from a short-lived range of small boxed sets with scenery, to a scale of 1:42, available in the early 1970s.

Although hollow-cast lead toy soldier manufacture on a large scale came to an end in 1966, when Britains stopped production, it was not long before a number of small firms started producing solid lead "traditional style" toy soldiers for collectors.

1-19 From Giles Brown's "Dorset Soldiers" range: a French supply column is ambushed in the desert. The figures are: (5-8) from set 26: Arabs; (1) set 27: Arabs on Camels; (11-13) set 32: Zouaves; (9-10) set 33: Turcos; (16-17) set 34: Foreign Legion; (14-15) set 52: Spahis; and (2-4) set 56: Mounted Arabs. A Maltese cart (18) is completed by a mule, mule-handler and stores.

20-27 From the range produced by Trophy Miniatures of South Wales: (20) French marine, China 1900; (21) British bluejacket, China 1900; (22) German East Asia Brigade, China 1900; (23) US infantry officer of 1900; (24) Sudanese infantryman of 1898; (25) British Camel Corps officer with binoculars; (26) bugler of the Ludhiana Sikhs; (27) Bonnie Prince Charlie.

28-33 From the "Kingcast" range produced by Peter Cowan, are shown figures from two sets of the 2nd Punjab Native Infantry of 1890: no. 1: Colours and Escort (28-29, 31-32), and no. 2: Infantry at Attention (30 and 33).

34-37 From Shamus Wade's discontinued Nostalgia range: (34) Ludhiana Sikh; (35) Indore artilleryman; (36) New South

Wales Lancer; (37) Havilder, 21st Bengal Infantry, c1815.

38-43 Some of the first traditional style figures were produced by the firm Blenheim Models: (38) standard-bearer of the 24th Foot, Zulu War; (39) infantryman of the 24th Foot, standing firing; (40-41) mule with ammunition boxes and mule handler; (42) trooper of the 12th Lancers at attention; (43) trooper of the City of London Yeomanry.

44-46 Bleu, Blanc et Rouge of Paris produce some very pleasing figures: (44) *cantiniere*, from a range of "Toy Town" figures; (45-46) French line infantry drummer and officer, c1900.

47-48 The shop Under Two Flags of London have their own range of figures, including this splendid

Man-of-War's boat (47). It has a crew of four sailors and four Royal Marine Light Infantry, and a good selection of stores (48).

49-65 From the author's own range, Bastion Models, are shown: (49-53) A 5in Howitzer of 1896, with Royal Artillery crew in foreign service order; (54) 51st Sikhs Punjab Frontier Force, China 1900; (55) German sailor, China 1900; (56) Japanese infantryman, China 1900; (57) Royal Marine Light Infantry, in tropical white uniform, China 1900; (58) Imperial Chinese regular infantry, 1900; (59) private, Hampshire Regiment, 1905; (60) British infantryman, 1914; (61) Belgian infantryman, 1914; (62) private, The Buffs, standing firing, Zulu War; (63) officer, The Buffs, Zulu

War; (64) private, Somerset Light Infantry, advancing, Zulu War; (65) private, 24th Foot, kneeling firing, Zulu War.

66-84 In 1973 Britains launched their "New Metal" soldiers, made of zinc alloy: (66) mounted Life Guard, introduced in 1984; (67) Horse Guard, being the same as (66) in blue; (68) H.M. The Queen, introduced in 1985; (69) Royal Canadian Mounted Policeman, also introduced in 1985; (70) dismounted Life Guard, introduced in 1974; (71) Horse Guard, the same casting as (70) but not introduced until 1983. (72-74) 1985 saw the introduction of these fine Scottish pipers of the Scots Guards, Gordons and Black Watch. (75) This Scots Guard was the first "New Metal" figure in

1973. (76) Yeoman of the Guard, introduced in 1974.

In 1983 Britains brought out their excellent marching Highlanders. (77-78) Officer and private of the Black Watch. (79-80) An officer and private of the Gordon Highlanders. (81-82) These Cameron Highlanders are from a limited run, only available in the USA. They have a more detailed paint finish, and the officer has a metal sword. (83-84) Argyll and Sutherland Highlanders, only available from the London Toy and Doll Museum in 1984-85.

Right: *In 1984 Britains brought out this special limited edition set of six Life Guards, with metal swords and scabbards and a more detailed paint finish.*

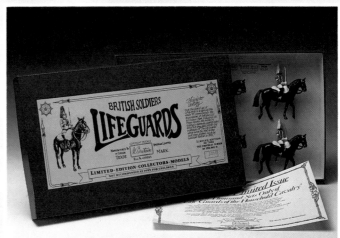

Bibliography

Colleccionismo de Soldados (Editorial Everest, Spain, 1978)
J. M. Allendesalazar

Model Soldiers (Charles Lett, 1973)
W. Y. Carman

Model Soldiers, a Collectors' Guide (Seeley Service, 1965)
The World Encyclopedia of Model Soldiers (Muller, 1981)
John G. Garratt

Toy Armies (Batsford), 1982)
Peter Johnson

Soldats de Plomb (Minute Print, Ohio, 1980)
Keester and Nelson

Collecting Old Toy Soldiers (Batsford, 1975)
Ian McKenzie

Metal Toys (Salamander, 1984)
Gordon Gardiner and Alistair Morris

Toy Soldiers (Shire, 1983)
British Toy Soldiers, 1893 to the Present (Arms amd Armour Press, 1985)
British Toy Soldiers, 1893-1932 (London, 1985)
James Opie

Model Tin Soldiers (Studio Vista, 1974)
Erwin Ortmann

The War Toys *Kriegsspielzeuge:* No 1,
The Story of Hausser-Elastolin (New Cavendish, 1979)
Reggie Polaine

Old British Model Soldiers 1893-1918 (Arms and Armour Press, 1970)
L. W. Richards

Bleisoldaten (Callwey, 1981)
Hans H. Roer

The Britains Collector's Checklist (private, USA)
Joanne and Ron Ruddell

A Collector's Guide to Britains Model Soldiers (Model and Allied Publications, 1980)
John Ruddle

Old Toy Soldier Newsletter
209 North Lombard, Oak Park, IL. 60302, USA

Toy Soldier Review
127 74th Street, North Bergen, N.J. 07047, USA

PRINTED IN BELGIUM BY
proost
INTERNATIONAL BOOK PRODUCTION